Leader's Guide 1

Friendship With God

The Incomparable Jesus

"Follow Me!"

Willow Creek Resources is a publishing partnership between Zondervan Publishing House and the Willow Creek Association. Willow Creek Resources will include drama sketches, small group curricula, training material, videos, and many other specialized ministry resources.

Willow Creek Association is an international network of churches ministering to the unchurched. Founded in 1992, the Willow Creek Association serves churches through conferences, seminars, regional roundtables, consulting, and ministry resource materials. The mission of the Association is to assist churches in reestablishing the priority and practice of reaching lost people for Christ through church ministries targeted to seekers.

For conference and seminar information please write to:

> Willow Creek Association
> P.O. Box 3188
> Barrington, Illinois 60011-3188

The Walking With God Series

Leader's Guide 1

Friendship With God
Developing Intimacy With God

The Incomparable Jesus
Experiencing the Power of Christ

"Follow Me!"
Walking With Jesus in Everyday Life

Don Cousins & Judson Poling

Zondervan PublishingHouse
Grand Rapids, Michigan

A Division of HarperCollins*Publishers*

The Walking With God Series Leader's Guide 1

Friendship With God:
   Developing Intimacy with God

The Incomparable Jesus:
   Experiencing the Power of Christ

"Follow Me!":
   Walking with Jesus in Everyday Life

The Walking With God Series Leader's Guide 2

Discovering the Church:
   Becoming Part of God's New Community

Building Your Church:
   Using Your Gifts, Time, and Resources

Impacting Your World:
   Becoming a Person of Influence

Published by Zondervan Publishing House, Grand Rapids, Michigan 49530.
Produced by The Livingstone Corporation. James C. Galvin, J. Michael Kendrick, Daryl J. Lucas, and Darcy J. Kamps, project staff.

ISBN 0-310-59203-8

Cover design: Mark Veldheer
Interior design: Catherine Bergstrom

Printed in the United States of America

97 98 99 / ❖ DH / 13 12 11 10 9 8

Preface

The *Walking With God Series* was developed as the curriculum for small groups at Willow Creek Community Church in South Barrington, Illinois. This innovative church has grown to over 15,000 in less than two decades, and the material here flows out of the vision and values of this dynamic ministry. Groups using these studies have produced many of the leaders, both staff and volunteer, throughout the church.

Associate Pastor Don Cousins wrote the first draft of this material and used it with his own small group. After testing it there, he revised it and passed his notes to Judson Poling, Director of Curriculum Development, who edited and expanded the outlines. Several pilot groups helped shape the material as it was being written and revised. A team of leaders labored through a line-by-line revision of these study guides over a year's span of time. Finally, these revisions were put into this new, more usable format.

Any church or group can use these studies in a relational context to help raise up devoted disciples. Group members who finish all six books will lay a solid foundation for a lifelong walk with God.

Contents

The Incomparable Jesus

Experiencing the Power of Christ

"Follow Me!"

Walking With Jesus In Everyday Life

Before You Start

At Willow Creek, we've long believed in the power of small groups—a few people coming together, sharing life experiences, and discussing God's Word in an intimate setting. While small groups may be formed for a variety of purposes, our single goal has been to produce disciples—fully devoted followers of Jesus Christ. As you will see, studying the Bible forms the foundation for the life change our small groups seek to produce. Now, to help you study God's Word in a format that encourages group discussion and allows you to make practical applications, we've developed the *Walking With God Series*.

The Target

When most groups come together, one of the first questions they discuss is, "What should we study?" Members express the interests, concerns, and needs on their minds at that time, and eventually they arrive at some consensus. While this method of curriculum selection has the advantage of addressing felt needs of the group members, it doesn't necessarily accomplish what God wants to see happen in the lives of the members. It would be better to ask questions such as, "What goals are we trying to reach? How should people be different after the small group ends? What results should group leaders be held accountable for? In other words, what target are we all trying to hit?"

The *Walking With God Series* was designed "backwards." That is, we started at the end and worked our way to the beginning. First we identified the characteristics of a mature disciple of Christ. Over time, we refined our picture and developed this target to describe the characteristics of this "fully devoted follower":

A Disciple Is One Who . . .

- Walks with God
- Lives the Word
- Contributes to the work
- Impacts the world

A Christian who *walks with God* has a personal relationship with Jesus and lives in step with the Holy Spirit. A Christian who *lives the Word* studies and applies the Bible to all areas of life. A Christian who *contributes to the work* uses his or her talents to help the growth and ministry of the local church. Finally, a Christian who *impacts the world* is one prepared and eager for personal evangelism.

Having a clear target made it easier to design a curriculum that would hit the mark. The six books in the series correspond to these four aspects of a mature Christian:

Walks with God	1. *Friendship With God*
Lives the Word	2. *The Incomparable Jesus*, and 3. *"Follow Me!"*
Contributes to the work	4. *Discovering the Church*, and 5. *Building Your Church*
Impacts the world	6. *Impacting Your World*

If the characteristics we identified are similar to what you hope to develop in your group members, then this material will help you reach your goal of leading followers of Christ to maturity.

The Series

The *Walking With God Series* is actually a two-track curriculum. The first track covers what happens in the group meetings. Discussion questions, outlines, and leader's notes are included to help that process. The second track is the homework, which is, in effect, personal devotions—Quiet Times. Discussions that happen in the group meetings open up new truth or reinforce lessons learned; the homework builds into members' lives personal habits for walking with God that can last a lifetime. Getting group members to do the quiet time track is very important because it is the pattern for what follows after the group ends.

The series includes six study guides:

1. Friendship With God

A look at our reason for living—our relationship with God—and the practical ways to make that relationship all it can be.

2. The Incomparable Jesus

A richly detailed study of the life of Jesus that begins with the Old Testament prophecies concerning his life and continues through the New Testament accounts of his miracles and parables.

3. "Follow Me!"

A continuation of the study of the life of Christ that focuses on his lordship in our lives and closely examines his betrayal, death, and resurrection.

4. Discovering the Church

A look at how God has brought us into an amazing new community of people—the church.

5. Building Your Church

An exploration of how to build up the body of Christ through serving and giving, with special attention given to spiritual gifts.

6. Impacting Your World

Practical studies to help communicate the life-changing message of Christ to others on an everyday basis.

In developing these studies, we've attempted to be practical, creative, and fun. A group member will nearly always consider the small group worthwhile when he or she draws personal, specific applications from the study and shares a bond with other members. Conversely, a person will have little enthusiasm or loyalty when studies become impersonal and routine. A good curriculum both avoids tedium and encourages people to share their ideas. Christians grow when they interact with one another and increase their understanding of the Bible. This material strives to promote both. It is also "adjustable"—group leaders with newer believers can "scale down" material to a corresponding level, while other groups with more mature believers can take advantage of the additional study questions provided with most studies.

Perhaps the feature of the *Walking With God Series* your group will find most valuable is its emphasis on the discipline of *quiet time*—the believer's regular sessions of personal Bible study and prayer. Your group will someday be over, and members will no longer do "homework." Whether your group members walk with God or not will depend on whether they have embraced the discipline of regular prayer and study in the Word. Knowing this, we made the personal quiet time the homework for each study rather than having group members simply fill in answers on a worksheet to be discussed at the next meeting.

Each member should be held accountable to complete the assignment. Since the assignments are both simple and meaningful, group members should not find it difficult to complete and benefit from them. You need to reinforce the value of this approach so that your people will become disciples who walk with Jesus as a way of life.

When your group members have completed all six studies in the *Walking With God Series*, they will have built a solid, spiritual foundation for their lives. They will have simple tools for taking additional steps in their spiritual journey. May God bless you as lead your group in his ways.

Why Small Groups?

Ever since the garden of Eden, God has longed for it to happen.

- With lots of time and no in-laws to interfere, newlyweds Adam and Eve should have fallen right into it—but their fall was in another direction.

- Abraham and his family were called out from their homeland to establish a new country that would display it—but the history of Israel is a failure in this area on a national scale.

- Jesus clearly tried to get it going among his followers—only to have them exhibit the status-seeking, self-serving agenda of the world around them.

- Paul, too, worked hard to get young churches to commit to it—but pagan values die hard, even among saints.

So, what has God been calling people to try? What does he want for us? The Bible explains that God has been reaching out to wayward, wandering souls since the beginning of human history. We've all been resisting his pull, but still he continues his work. His ongoing saga could be called "The Great Reconnection"—first, between us and him, and then between us and each other. In a word, God left heaven to bring us "community."

Families are supposed to be the first place we experience this gift. If things went according to plan, from there we'd live it out in the church, and even in society to some extent. Our work should be done through community. Much of our play could be in community. Our worship would leap up to heaven out of community. Our togetherness would not replace our need for solitude but would complement it—and we wouldn't use our desire to be alone as a way to avoid community.

Unfortunately, that isn't the way life works for most people. Many of our families are not as close-knit as we wish they could be. In the same way, churches try but seldom reach their potential. And our society, without dependence on God, can never hope to find what it so desperately needs.

A new movement, however, is giving many people hope. Within churches, people are gathering in smaller numbers to share their lives with each other. Men are getting up a little earlier once a week to meet for breakfast and Bible study. Young moms are putting the kids down for a nap and gathering with others to feed their souls and share their struggles. Couples are meeting in homes a few times a month to discuss truth instead of just passively listening to it. People are experiencing a new learning environment, but more than that, they're learning about a new "living" environment—they're tasting the benefits of small groups as a way of life.

The *Walking With God Series* is not just another resource for people who want to learn something new—it's a workbook for experiencing a new quality of life in the context of a small group. The program is designed to be done in groups because of our commitment to the value that *group life is the foundation of church life.*

Why are small groups so important to the church? Simply because of what they produce. If you don't need any of the following, then don't bother with small groups. But if your church is looking for better ways to develop the characteristics listed here, invest your time and resources to promote small groups.

- **Small groups produce disciples**—People grow best in a loving environment, not in an academic one. Small groups are the right size for personal care, yet challenging enough to promote growth.

- **Small groups produce leaders**—When people experience the life of Christ transforming them, they want to share it with others. They become leaders because in a small group they are seen for who they are, can make character changes more effectively, and have an example to pass along to the next generation of Christians.

- **Small groups produce workers**—People who know their spiritual gift and want to use it will become involved instead of remaining spectators.

- **Small groups produce contributors**—People who know about the biblical teaching on giving and see others "laying up treasures in heaven" will discover the adventure of investing in Kingdom work.

- **Small groups can reach the lost**—As people experience Christian community and see God's heart for reaching non-churched people, they respond by becoming people of influence in their personal circles.

- **Small groups are nurturing**—With the decay of families so prevalent, small groups can help rebuild broken lives and act as a support for people trying to stop the cycle of dysfunction.

- **Small groups are fun**—Some of the best time adults have with one another can result from small group functions. Whether in the group meeting or during other planned activities, play is an important part of building the community God wants us to experience.

If we were to rank the above list, we would put "making disciples" at the top. The Great Commission in Matthew 28:18-20 is not primarily about evangelism—it is about making disciples. Jesus did not tell us to pass on what he commanded—he specifically said to teach others to *obey* what he commanded. All of the other benefits flow out of helping people be disciples; meet that pressing need, and mature disciples will be there to meet all the others.

The Right Match of People

Most small groups will fall far short of their potential if just anyone is allowed to join. Care must be taken to arrange for the right mix of people for each group. This often overlooked step is critical because over time the group members will become like family. Good leaders pay attention to the importance of bringing together the right people for each group. Three keys to the good selection of small group members are affinity, availability, and teachability.

First, make sure each member of the group is "hand-picked"—selected for his or her strong potential for a friendship to develop between you and the other group members. We call this the principle of affinity. There are times to celebrate diversity in the body of Christ, but a small group requires people to spend a lot of time together. They must like to be with each other or the meetings will become a "have to" instead of a "want to." Plenty of diversity will come out even when you feel a strong potential for friendship, so don't be embarrassed to select people with whom you will enjoy investing the time to build a relationship.

Second, group members should understand that they are to place a premium on meeting together on a weekly basis. A commitment to making the time available is vital to ensuring the effectiveness of the group. So impress on each person that while sacrifices may be necessary, the small group experience will be worth it in the long run.

Third, you need to gauge as accurately as possible whether each person desires spiritual growth and instruction. Casual Christians quench the enthusiasm of the leader and the group, and only those with a hunger to know God will respond readily to the weekly assignments in these study guides.

The Role of the Leader

Children don't grow into adulthood through correspondence courses, and believers don't become disciples that way either. What a child needs is an example to follow—and that's exactly the pattern of discipleship. Consider what Paul says to his disciple Timothy, and also how he says it: "You then, my son, be strong in the grace that is in Christ Jesus. And the things you have heard me say in the presence of many witnesses entrust to reliable men who will also be qualified to teach others" (2 Timothy 2:2). Paul had been a "father" to Timothy, and that pattern of affectionate teaching should be followed in Timothy's ministry as well. This passing on of truth in a relational context is foundational to a church. It is why small groups are so vital to a growing ministry, because that is the place learning and loving occur so effectively.

But more than truth gets passed on in a small group. Although the leader's role is to guide discussion, as an example, the leader, along with other members, share something of great worth—their lives. "We loved you so much that we were delighted to share with you not only the gospel of God but our lives as well, because you had become so dear to us" (1 Thessalonians 2:8). Small groups cannot be reduced to another "class" or they will fail to achieve one of their key objectives: sharing truth about ourselves, not just truth from the pages of Scripture. The leader must model vulnerability and guide the meetings in such a way that everyone participates at this level. This commitment to talking about life as it is, as well as moving toward what we want it to be, is why we're not exaggerating when we say small groups are about *life change.* Good content can't penetrate a closed heart, but an open life, having the truth of God gradually shine in every area, will be transformed. The leader's main role is to foster such an environment and show the way by example.

Every leader will probably have his or her own style of preparing and then leading, and that is as it should be. But a few simple steps should be followed by all leaders.

1. **Don't expect the study to work without preparation**. Going cold into a group meeting, expecting the discussion questions alone to carry the time, will not achieve what you desire. Be sure you've looked over the lesson and studied the answers provided so you know how to steer the discussion. Provide some insights of your own, and even add follow-up questions you think of. Consider the spiritual stage of your people and customize accordingly.

2. **Prepare with the "Purpose" and "Bottom Line" in mind.** Groups get off track when discussion meanders along interesting but tangential "rabbit trails." The "Purpose" statement and "Bottom Line" can help you see where questions should lead and keep you from trying to explore the many topics that could come up in a meeting but that would be ancillary to the goals for that meeting. If group members want to explore other issues, schedule time outside your ordinary meeting time or suggest optional reading. The *Walking With God Series* was not designed to be a collection of electives that merely satisfy spiritual curiosity. Instead, it was written to help those who use it lay a biblical foundation for lifelong discipleship. Don't frustrate your group by allowing meetings to degenerate into haphazard, "all-things-to-all-people" gabfests.

3. **Prepare to lead *people*, not just meetings.** It's easy to let stimulating content or relevant biblical information be the focus of your thoughts during your preparation time. But leaders must always be thinking, "How will this truth or that question affect each individual group member?" The goal of a meeting is never the delivery of information alone. The goal is always group

members receiving information and improving their connections to each other and to God. Don't be satisfied thinking, "I know what all this means, and I'll be able to explain it." Ask, "How can I pull everyone in to *feel* the significance of this topic to their lives?"

4. Pray for your group members. All of our plans to bring about life change will be useless without the Holy Spirit's work both in the preparation and during the meetings. Commit the people and their needs to God through prayer. Pray for your own abilities to lead discussion effectively, without dominating but without abdicating either. Pray that God will be free to interrupt plans, but also that he will protect good plans from the competition of less significant matters. So many of God's promises are tied to fruitfulness in ministry—thank God for his desire to help you bear fruit in members' lives, and ask that the work you're doing continue unhindered.

How to Lead a Meeting

Leading a small group—especially for the first time—can make you feel both nervous and excited. Keep in mind that your role is simply to get everyone involved by asking questions and encouraging people to respond. Small group leaders actually lead more than they teach. It's everyone's responsibility to make the group work by participating. A good leader draws everyone in and everyone out. The suggestions listed here can help you be a more effective leader.

Before the Study

1. Before the first meeting, make sure everyone has his or her own study guide.

2. Ask God to help you understand and apply the study to your own life.

3. Carefully work through each question and the leader's notes for each study.

4. Pray for each person in the group.

During the Study

1. Begin on time. This will reinforce the value of honoring each other's time.

2. Encourage participation and make sure the group knows that these studies are designed to be discussions, not lectures.

3. The questions in the guide are designed to be used just as they are written, but you may wish to restate them in your own words. Try not to change the meaning of the questions, however.

4. Avoid answering your own questions. If necessary, rephrase a question until it is clearly understood. Don't discourage participation by giving the impression that you will be doing most of the talking.

5. Encourage two or three responses to question. Try to avoid letting the same person respond to question after question.

6. Affirm the worth of any response and never reject answers outright. If an answer is clearly wrong, ask the person what led him or her to that conclusion or let the group respond to the answer.

7. End on time. This shows respect for the schedules of your group members.

After the Study

1. Call or visit any group members who would like to talk further with you about any issue.

2. Complete the homework assigned to the group members.

3. Schedule time to prepare for the next study.

Group Members and Their Walk with God

The most strategic contribution that you can make to your group members' lives is to help them learn to feed themselves from God's Word. "Give a man a fish, and you feed him for a day; teach a man to fish, and you feed him for a lifetime." What happens in your meetings is important, but think of the long-term effects if every member learns to get alone regularly with God for prayer and Bible study. Rather than force small group members to choose between homework and meeting with God, we made the appointments with God the homework. That way, they have a better chance to adopt the disciplines as a way of life.

The members of your group may resist this approach and wonder why they have to do the independent work and why you take time each meeting to share what was learned. Remind them and yourself that the purpose of this program is to build lifelong habits, not to take a crash course in Christianity. Remember cramming for exams in college? Nobody wants to do that their whole life. Yet to some group members the assignments could feel just like that. Doing the homework should affect them positively—unlike "all-nighters" from college days! Then, by taking time during meetings to talk about what they've learned, people experience the joy of sharing their discoveries. The value of self-feeding is reinforced. When the process of learning isn't extreme, members will continue the pattern they have established *after* your group is done. We believe the ultimate success of your group and of this curriculum depends on holding people accountable to this pattern of meeting with God on their own.

One of our greatest concerns as we developed this material was to help group members establish a lifelong habit of regular devotional times. Generally, busy people don't have time for both lesson preparations and personal devotions. So we wanted to create homework assignments that were appointments with God—no more and no less.

How to Do the Homework

After every study, you will find a three-part assignment: a passage of Scripture to be studied, a list of prayer emphases, and a Scripture memory verse. Group members are to set aside time on at least three occasions during the week to meet alone with God and do the assignments. (Of course, they may want to meet with God more often or do more than the assigned material—that's up to them. These assignments represent a minimum for group participation.) They may repeat the assignment three times, or do a third of it each time—the instructions will often spell out which way is best.

Some group members may choose not to memorize verses with the rest of the group. Though this part of the assignment is highly recommended, it's not mandatory—each group (or member) will need to determine expectations. The rest of the assignment is required of everyone. The prayer emphases are pretty straightforward—members can pray about more than what is suggested, but the topics represent a few subjects everyone should focus on. The chapters of Scripture assigned should be read, and members should take notes. We propose a simple two-column format: list on the left side *observations* you note about the verse (or paragraph) and list on the right side *applications* you intend to make based on your observations. Naturally, members may want to do more than this and utilize other methods and tools at their disposal (especially in the first book where assignments are so basic). Again, our point is to give people a practical benchmark for their personal times with God and help them have successful experiences. New Christians need time to grow into the habit of a quiet time, and believers of all spiritual ages are probably busy enough to appreciate realistic demands on their schedules.

A special journal has been developed to go along with the *Walking With God Series* called the *Walking With God Journal.* It has introductory material about establishing regular quiet times and plenty of blank pages on which to write out the homework for this series. We would encourage group members to get one of these books for recording their assignments so their work can be organized and loose pages don't get lost. Members can obtain additional books as they fill up the ones they have. Although any blank paper can be used to do the assignments, these books give members a simple format to help establish the lifelong habit of time with God. The journal can continue to be used after the group is over, making the discipline more permanent. You can purchase the *Walking With God Journal* at your local Christian bookstore.

Basic Format for a Meeting

The *Walking With God Series* can be used equally well in a small group that meets from an hour and one-half to two hours, or in a more traditional class setting with only one hour available. The study format can be adapted to fit the needs of shorter sessions simply by eliminating the Opener and Review sections and beginning with the Purpose section. The approximate time required for each section is listed below.

Overview

- The overview is meant to give the leader a thumbnail sketch of the theme of a particular study.

- It usually gives advice on how to impress important ideas on group members.

Prayer (1-5 minutes)

- Start your group on time!

- You should offer the opening prayer or select a group member to do so.

- Avoid bringing up personal concerns at this time; concentrate instead on spiritual preparation for the study.

- Let the prayer set the tone for the meeting—don't take it lightly.

Opener (15-20 minutes)

- The opener is usually a question or fill-in-the-blank statement. It is meant to stimulate conversation and to open people up for further discussion. It can be serious or light.

- Sometimes one opener will be enough, but feel free to use two, depending on the personality of the group and the time you have available.

- Feel free to make up your own questions if that will help your group learn more about one another.

Review (20-25 minutes)

- The review consists of three parts: Bible study, prayer, and (if you choose to include it) Scripture memory. Each part will have been assigned to the group the previous week.

- Emphasize accountability. Follow up with people who have trouble completing their assignments.

- Encourage people to make specific applications from their assignments to their own life situations.

- Follow up on prayer assignments. Usually, just sharing one aspect of what they prayed for will be all that time will allow.

Purpose (3-5 minutes)

- Either you or a group member should read aloud the short paragraphs found in the Purpose section.

- Emphasize the purpose statement so that your group members have a clear idea of the learning objective for the study.

Study (50-60 minutes)

- This section is the core of the study, integrating Bible study, teaching, and discussion in a question-and-answer format.

- You should do your best to draw out and include everyone in the discussion.

- Have group members take notes and write answers to questions in their study guides.

Bottom Line (1-2 minutes)

- Have group members write the Bottom Line in their books as you read it to them.

Your Walk with God (3-5 minutes)

- This section contains the "homework" for the next study. Like the Review, it consists of Bible study, prayer, and Scripture memory.

- Make sure the group understands what is expected of them.

- Hold group members accountable for completing the assignments.

Prayer (1-5 minutes)

- You should conclude each study with prayer.

- Introduce variety here—for one session, have one member close in prayer; for another, have the entire group pray a short prayer; for another, read a Psalm aloud together, and so on.

- Be sensitive to those who are uncomfortable with conversational prayer.

- Serve refreshments afterward, if you desire. While beverages may be appropriate during the meeting, we recommend waiting until the end of the meeting to serve food so that discussion is not disrupted.

On Your Own

- This section provides supplemental material that your members should read before the next meeting.

Getting Started—Your First Group Meetings

We realize that not every group will want to start in the same place. Although the books in the *Walking With God Series* were designed sequentially, they do not have to be done in that order to be effective. Wherever you start your group, it is a good idea to begin relationally. We've included two studies in this leader's guide called "First Impressions" and "Getting to Know You" to be used as the first two meetings when you begin your small group. You do not need to do these at the beginning of each study guide, but they are a good place to start for your first gatherings, especially if group members don't know each other well.

Throughout the duration of your small group, it is also a good idea to take a break from time to time and do either relational or social activities together. Seeing each other in a nonstructured or fun environment is not an add-on to the discipling process—it's a necessary part of it. Jesus shared much of his life with his disciples—working together and traveling together as well as talking to them.

Stages in The Life of a Small Group

One certainty you will face in the life of any small group is change. All small groups go through phases at various points in their existence. By recognizing these stages, you can be more prepared for them when they come. You can also avoid feeling that you've done something wrong when these changes in your group appear. You're not a bad leader—these things just happen!

Stage One: Honeymoon

In this stage, excitement is evident as the group begins. People are motivated to grow and learn. They prepare for the study. They look up to your leadership and invite you to hold them accountable. Everyone seems to be getting along and expresses confidence that something good is going to come out of this group.

Unfortunately, people in this stage often have unrealistic expectations. They may expect too much of themselves and of your leadership. Without realizing it, they may come to believe that you can solve their problems and do their growing for them.

The main thing to do during this stage is . . . enjoy it! Take the group along this road as far as they'll go. Like any honeymoon, it will be joyful—and temporary.

Stage Two: Disillusionment

Some would call this stage the "reality" or "transitional" stage. Suddenly members realize that accountability and growth are a challenge, and getting together regularly is a lot harder than they thought. When members realize reality probably won't match their expectations, they grow restless, frustrated, even angry. Some individuals may even challenge your leadership and authority.

It is important to negotiate this stage without becoming overly defensive or frustrated. Some leaders get to this stage and suddenly think they are no longer qualified to lead. But don't take expressions of dissatisfaction personally. Often the leader is simply the most convenient target for free-floating frustration.

Of course, there is a difference between an ebb in the group's enthusiasm and wanton rebellion or a divisive spirit. The latter behavior is a cancer that will eventually destroy your group. It must be dealt with lovingly but firmly. Be aware also that building a meaningful relationship takes time and effort, and as the relationship grows, it will inevitably have to endure some awkward stages. A "perfect" small group experience with no problems at all is probably a group in which no real change takes place.

Stage Three: Growth

At this stage, the group begins to synthesize its values, strengths, gifts, and temperaments. The initial issues have been resolved, and the group moves into a more productive period, eagerly anticipating the future. Established goals are achieved and new ones set.

As the leader, you must remind the others that your small group will end someday. Challenge members to think about God's plans for their future beyond the group. Also, be alert for boredom and complacency. Are you customizing the studies to meet their needs? Without lowering standards, can you share some of the leadership of parts of the discussion? Look for new challenges, new goals, and new outreach to keep your group members stretched.

Stage Four: Culmination

As the group comes to an end, each member will start to reflect on what has been accomplished. The termination period of a small group is both exciting, as members contemplate what lies beyond the group experience, and sad, as members contemplate life without weekly visits with these close friends. Be prepared for expressions of grief and even anger. Because friendships have become so tight, people may not want to stop meeting together. You'll spare a lot of unnecessary hurt feelings if you announce throughout your studies that the group has been set up to last only for the duration of the curriculum; you won't continue meeting indefinitely. Don't suddenly drop on them the news that, after meeting two years, the group is going to end in three weeks.

When Paul was leaving the church at Ephesus, the saints there wept as they embraced and kissed him (Acts 20:37-38). The Ephesians didn't want to see Paul go. Undoubtedly, it was also difficult for Paul to leave these close brothers and sisters. Yet God was calling him to greater things, and the Ephesian church understood the calling. The pain of separation was there, but the higher goals of the gospel overcame their own desires. The same principle applies to us in disciplemaking. Besides, what greater joy is there for a discipler than to see his or her pupils go on to disciple others? Is there any higher calling?

Praying for Your Small Group Members

My work was to plant the seed in your hearts, and Apollos' work was to water it, but it was God, not we, who made the garden grow in your hearts.
1 Corinthians 3:6 (TLB)

One of the most fruitful works we can do on behalf of the people we disciple is to pray for them. God's power comes to bear and our work takes on a new dimension of spirituality. Thoughts and wishes for our small group members are turned into specific requests that are heard by God and answered. Other aspects of our leadership may be more visible and have more immediate results—yet no other activity produces as much lasting fruit as praying.

The Bible provides many examples of prayers that can serve as models for people in leadership of a small group. Sometimes, we can use these prayers almost word for word as we pray for a group member. Consider the following prayers of Paul. In them, you may find words and phrases that express what you would like to pray about for your group members.

Ephesians 1:15-19—*For this reason, ever since I heard about your faith in the Lord Jesus and your love for all the saints, I have not stopped giving thanks for you, remembering you in my prayers. I keep asking that the God of our Lord Jesus Christ, the glorious Father, may give you the Spirit of wisdom and revelation, so that you may know him better. I pray also that the eyes of your heart may be enlightened in order that you may know the hope to which he has called you, the riches of his glorious inheritance in the saints, and his incomparably great power for us who believe.*

Philippians 1:3-6, 9-11—*I thank my God every time I remember you. In all my prayers for all of you, I always pray with joy because of your partnership in the gospel from the first day until now, being confident of this, that he who began a good work in you will carry it on to completion until the day of Christ Jesus.*

And this is my prayer: that your love may abound more and more in knowledge and depth of insight, so that you may be able to discern what is best and may be pure and blameless until the day of Christ, filled with the fruit of righteousness that comes through Jesus Christ—to the glory and praise of God.

Colossians 1:9-12—*For this reason, since the day we heard about you, we have not stopped praying for you and asking God to fill you with the knowledge of his will through all spiritual wisdom and understanding. And we pray this in order that you may live a life worthy of the Lord and may please him in every way: bearing fruit in every good work, growing in the knowledge of God, being strengthened with all power according to his glorious might so that you may have great endurance and patience, and joyfully giving thanks to the Father, who has qualified you to share in the inheritance of the saints in the kingdom of light.*

1 Thessalonians 3:9-13—*How can we thank God enough for you in return for all the joy we have in the presence of our God because of you? Night and day we pray most earnestly that we may see you again and supply what is lacking in your faith.*

Now may our God and Father himself and our Lord Jesus clear the way for us to come to you. May the Lord make your love increase and overflow for each other and for everyone else, just as ours does for you. May he strengthen your hearts so that you will be blameless and holy in the presence of our God and Father when our Lord Jesus comes with all his holy ones.

2 Thessalonians 1:11-12—*With this in mind, we constantly pray for you, that our God may count you worthy of his calling, and that by his power he may fulfill every good purpose of yours and every act prompted by your faith. We pray this so that the name of our Lord Jesus may be glorified in you, and you in him, according to the grace of our God and the Lord Jesus Christ.*

Philemon 4-6—*I always thank my God as I remember you in my prayers, because I hear about your faith in the Lord Jesus and your love for all the saints. I pray that you may be active in sharing your faith, so that you will have a full understanding of every good thing we have in Christ.*

Sometimes, categories can help you organize your prayers for your gorup members. Throughout the discipleship material, we have stressed the four marks of a fully devoted follower of Christ:

A Disciple Is One Who . . .

- Walks with God
- Lives the Word
- Contributes to the work
- Impacts the world.

These four marks of maturity are a good way to pray for each person in your group. Use scriptural principles whenever possible as you identify matters to bring before the Lord. Consider the following references to get you started:

Walks with God

Colossians 2:5-7—*For though I am absent from you in body, I am present with you in spirit and delight to see how orderly you are and how firm your faith in Christ is.*

So then, just as you received Christ Jesus as Lord, continue to live in him, rooted and built up in him, strengthened in the faith as you were taught, and overflowing with thankfulness.

Example: Lord, help Jim to be more stable in his faith. Help him be disciplined with his quiet time. Help him trust you and not be afraid to depend on you even though he is so independent by nature. Help him to be a more grateful man, one who takes opportunities throughout the day to pause and say thanks to you.

Lives the Word

Colossians 3:16-17—*Let the word of Christ dwell in you richly as you teach and admonish one another with all wisdom, and as you sing psalms, hymns and spiritual songs with gratitude in your hearts to God. And whatever you do, whether in word or deed, do it all in the name of the Lord Jesus, giving thanks to God the Father through him.*

Example: Heavenly Father, I'm so glad you gave us the Bible. I pray you'll help Jane get a stronger hold on your Word and that you will get a stronger hold on her. Help her to be thankful for the guidance you've given through the Scriptures instead of being angry that you "restrict" her with commandments.

Contributes to the work

Colossians 1:28-29—*We proclaim him, admonishing and teaching everyone with all wisdom, so that we may present everyone perfect in Christ. To this end I labor, struggling with all his energy, which so powerfully works in me.*

Example: Dear God, I thank you for bringing Tom to yourself. Help him to use his skills and talents for your glory. Give him a vision of building your kingdom instead of just building his own little empire. Help him someday work as hard for your cause as he does now for his own company.

Impacts the world

Colossians 4:5-6—*Be wise in the way you act toward outsiders; make the most of every opportunity. Let your conversation be always full of grace, seasoned with salt, so that you may know how to answer everyone.*

Example: Jesus, please show Sue what she can do to reach her sister for you. I know she carries around so much concern for her spiritual well-being. Help her to know what to say. And also help her at work. Give her the words so her witness can be natural and have a positive effect. Don't let her miss the opportunities you give her.

There is a time to talk people about God, and there is a time to talk to God about people. Jesus spent time talking directly to his disciples. He also spent time talking to others while the disciples listened. But one of the most important works he did—and one of the most important works we can do—was to spend time talking to his heavenly Father. When the discipleship process is compete, it may turn out that the moments on our knees did more good than any of our teaching.

A Word about Walk and Talk

Therefore go and make disciples of all nations, baptizing them in the name of the Father and of the Son and of the Holy Spirit, and teaching them to obey everything I have commanded you. And surely I am with you always, to the very end of the age. Matthew 28:19-20

If the dispensing of information alone could change people, Jesus might have given us a slightly different Great Commission. He could have said "Teaching them everything I have commanded you." But that's not how he left it. He said, "Teaching them *to obey* everything I have commanded you." Those two words are the difference between Christian education and making disciples.

Two important ingredients in your leadership of the group should include what we call "walk" and "talk." Simply put, "talk" is that part of the small group experience where you talk about the Christian life. "Walk" is the part where people see you in action outside of the meeting, where they learn how to put their faith into action. Jesus taught the Twelve, but he also lived with them. He *talked* with them and *walked* with them.

Remember that leading a group involves sharing both your walk and talk. Plan social times with your group so they can see you in action in a variety of contexts. You should plan some time to get together at least once or twice per quarter. If you can, meet with each person individually outside of the group meeting. It's one thing to talk about the Christian life. It's another to live it out in front of them. Jesus did both. For maximum impact as a small group leader, you also need to do both. Remember:

Walk without talk lacks understanding.

Talk without walk lacks power.

First Impressions

(A Recommended Meeting)

Overview

Before you begin the first study, we strongly recommend planning a social activity so that group members can meet each other informally. In some cases, the group members will be total strangers to each other, so this social activity is essential. In other cases, the group members may already know each other or have established friendships. Yet this kind of social activity is still a good way to start the small group.

This meeting is the first time the group gets together, so it is important for several reasons:

1. Group members will form their first impressions of each other. They will also be conscious of the impressions they *make*. Some people will probably be nervous—new experiences tend to make us anxious. Therefore, try to make everyone feel comfortable and relaxed.

2. The group will also form its first impressions of your leadership. Good planning, promptness, and courtesy on your part will allow the group to feel confident in your abilities. Conversely, inadequate preparation, sloppy organization, and a domineering attitude will negate any message you are trying to get across.

3. This meeting also sets the tone for the meetings to follow. The qualities that you want to emphasize throughout these studies should be evident at the first meeting. Your meetings should be *relational*—they should acknowledge that God works through people. Your meetings should also be *practical*—they should help people grow spiritually in the real world. Finally, your meetings should be *recreational*—they should convey the impression that its OK for Christians to have fun!

Activity

In a word, this first meeting is a social event. You should select a group activity that is:

- Mandatory—It is absolutely essential that every person in the group be there. If someone has to cancel at the last minute, either reschedule or plan a different event so that everyone is there. *This meeting is too important to have anyone miss.*

- Non-threatening—No one should be put on the spot or made to do something embarrassing.

- Neutral—Don't pick a place associated with "churchy" activities.

- Conversational—Don't choose a spectator event (such as a movie or concert) where group members have no opportunity to talk.

- Inclusive—The leader should be sensitive to draw everyone into the conversations.

- Casual—Formal attire usually stifles free sharing.

- Enjoyable—Allow individuals to express humor or pleasure.

- Inexpensive—Be considerate of people's budgets.

- Creative—Add extra touches to show group members that they matter to you.

Once you decide on an activity, notify group members as to its date, time, cost, and other considerations. You may want to plan a surprise that is revealed once the event begins (keeping in mind that it should be low-key and nonthreatening). Traveling together to the activity rather than meeting there can get your time off to a fun start. And be sure to end at the designated time. You want the group to have a good time and look forward to their next meeting together. A successful first outing will go a long way toward strengthening the commitment of the group.

Following this social event, your first formal meeting should continue this process of helping group members get to know each other. See the section "Getting to Know You" for instructions on how to run this next meeting for your group. As you leave your social event, be sure everyone knows the time and place for the next get-together.

Note: If after this first meeting it is clear that some people do not get along or that one person in particular is producing conflict, it may be wise to place those who don't fit in another group (if possible).

Ideas for Your Social Event

1. Visit a museum

2. Go to a dinner theater

3. Attend a sporting event

4. Go bowling

5. Go to an unusual restaurant

6. Have a progressive dinner or potluck

7. Hike on a trail or through a forest preserve

8. Go shopping

9. Throw a Super Bowl party

10. Take a boat or train ride

11. Visit a lake or the ocean

12. Have a picnic

13. Organize a bicycle outing

You can also find ideas for social events by checking a regional magazine, your local newspaper, or by calling your state bureau of tourism.

Enjoy your outing!

Getting to Know You

(A Recommended Meeting)

Overview

Before you start working through the study guides together, you may want first to hold a meeting to help group members get to know each other better. This meeting is a relational exercise specifically designed for new groups.

Relational Exercise

Important Guidelines

As you get together for this first meeting in a home, be careful to observe the following suggestions:

- Meet in your home or in another controlled setting. This allows you to control interruptions such as the phone, children, pets, and so on.

- Meeting times should be conducive to people's schedules and relative alertness.

- Meet only when everyone can be there. This is an important rule to follow for the first two meetings. Afterwards, just try your best to encourage 100 percent attendance.

- No Bible is necessary for this meeting, but group members must bring their calendars so that future meetings can be scheduled (plan them at least four to six weeks in advance). Provide paper and pens for everyone this week, though next week they'll need to bring their own.

- Meet in a comfortable setting—a family room or den is ideal.

- Serve refreshments if you like, but save snacks and other foods for the end of the meeting to minimize distractions.

- People should be seated in a circle, but it should be adjusted so nobody is too close or too far apart.

- Start on time. It is important to establish from the very beginning that the group will begin on time. If members want to have a time of informal conversation, have them come fifteen minutes early.

Twenty Questions

Group members don't need to write out these questions, but as you read them they should jot down an answer to each one. Be sure to let people have fun with this—it can go a long way toward building rapport.

After all the questions have been read and answers written, go back to the first question and have them share their responses. When you move to the next question, have a new person begin the round of answers—that way, no one is put on the spot to be first for every question. Also, don't force anyone to answer a question if he or she does not want to do so. The only exception to this is the last question—make sure everyone shares his or her answer at the end.

1. My favorite movie of all time is _____.

2. My idea of a great vacation is _____.

3. Two of my pet peeves are _____ and _____.

4. It's very difficult for me to discipline myself when it comes to _____.

5. The one thing most people misunderstand about me is _____.

6. My favorite food is _____.

7. The greatest challenge I have ever faced is _____.

8. One thing I really appreciate about my spouse (or a close friend) is _____.

9. If I could change one thing about myself, I'd change _____.

10. The toughest period of my life was _____.

11. While growing up I saw God as _____.

12. One thing I have learned about myself in the past year is _____.

13. One thing I have learned about God in the past year is _____.

14. Before I die, I would like to _____.

15. If I could visit any era of history, I would visit _____.

16. The one aspect of my spiritual life I would like to strengthen is _____.

17. One character quality I would like to develop is _____.

18. My favorite childhood memory is _____.

19. My favorite leisure activity is _____.

2 20. The two most important benefits that I would like from my involvement in this small group are _____ and _____.

Schedule

Finally, discuss the schedule of meetings in the weeks to come:

- Dates, times, places—schedule the next six meetings.

- What to bring: Bible (NIV), pen or pencil, their own copy of *Friendship With God* or other book in the series.

- Reiterate the need to start on time. Commitment to a small group means they have agreed to show up, show up *on time*, and show up *prepared*.

- The homework for the next study is simply to come with the proper materials.

- If group member would like to give some thought to the general topic of next week's study, give them the following questions to consider:

1. Think about a time when someone tried to establish a friendship with you. What did that person do to initiate this relationship with you?

2. For what reasons would God be a friend worth having? What are some of the ways he has tried to initiate a relationship with you?

Prayer

End your time together by leading in a short prayer. (Only you should pray, unless you know the group would feel comfortable with conversational prayer.)

Friendship With God

Developing Intimacy with God

Introduction

At its core, Christianity is Christ. Christians embrace a Person, not merely a philosophy. It is not knowing about his teaching so much as it is knowing him. The greatest misunderstanding about Christianity today, even in the church, is the perception that God's bottom-line requirements are deeds to be done and beliefs to be believed. The Christ who spoke is bypassed for the things he spoke; the Guide is left behind for the guidance; the Commander is ignored in the carrying out of commands. The *Walking With God Series* addresses this problem by encouraging the Christian to develop a relationship with the living God.

This series is based on the belief that a disciple is one who

- walks with God

- lives the Word

- contributes to the work

- impacts the world

So we begin this curriculum with a study of that essential relationship (*Friendship With God*). The next two study guides are an examination of the life of Jesus (*The Incomparable Jesus* and *"Follow Me!"*). After that, we learn of our place in the gathering of believers known as the church (*Discovering the Church* and *Building Your Church*). Finally, we conclude by learning ways to make our mark for his kingdom (*Impacting Your World*).

We do not intend to bury people in mountains of theological information. Our interest lies in transforming hearts. We'd readily recommend two years of a small group experience that truly caused people to know God over twenty years of "Christian education" that rendered them all but dead to the real world and the God who is willing to walk with them in it. Bible studies alone won't produce that change. Thus, we have designed the assignments as a subtle way of getting people to begin their own times alone with God. Ultimately, the success of this study will depend on how consistently you walk with God after the study is over.

A Friend
Worth Having

OVERVIEW

The purpose of this study is to help your group members understand what it means to relate to God in a personal way.

Your main goal as the leader of a small group is building Christ-like character into each member. This character development process begins with a personal relationship with Christ. The message that comes through loud and clear in this study is, "God *wants* to have a relationship with *you*," rather than "you *ought* to have a relationship with *him*."

Let your group members know that God is not only a friend worth having but also a friend who's already heard about them and wants to be close to them. God has already initiated an all-out effort to reach into their lives to get the relationship going.

PRAYER

Begin the meeting with a short prayer. This is what you should do first each week after everybody has arrived. It marks the formal beginning of every meeting.

OPENER

Say something like: **Let's begin by talking about the kind of week each of us has had.** Ask the first question, then go around the circle having each member

45

respond. You may want to be the first person to answer to help set a relaxed tone for the meeting.

The highlight of the past week for me was _____.

Then ask the second question and go around the circle again for response.

The lowlight of the past week for me was _____.

REVIEW

Since this is the first week of the study, there is no review.

PURPOSE

Have your group members open their books to the first study. Then read the introduction, or have one of the group members read it while the others follow along.

Suppose you have to choose between two people who want to go to dinner with you. The first person is very warm and takes a genuine interest in others. He listens attentively and is fun to be with. Those who develop a friendship with him want it to last a lifetime.

In contrast, the second person is aloof and demanding. He keeps most of his friends (if you could call them that) at a distance. The only time he calls is when he wants something from you. He's pretty unpredictable emotionally, and you never quite know where you stand with him. He wields considerable influence, but if it weren't for his power he probably wouldn't have any friends at all. If you're like most people, you'd rather have dinner with the first person.

Who is God like in your mind—the first person or the second? Unfortunately, many people have a distorted view of God's character. To them, he's much like the second person—distant and uncaring. Although he is powerful, he can't be counted on. The only real benefit in knowing him comes from occasional answers to prayer. No wonder people have a hard time relating to him! Who would want to cultivate a friendship like that?

If your view of God has been been colored by mistaken assumptions and erroneous ideas, it can be startling to learn that God longs to establish a close, intimate friendship with you. This study will help you understand what it means to relate to God in a personal way. Let this one truth sink in: *God is a Friend worth having.*

What are some necessary ingredients for building a relationship with another person?

> Draw out the following ideas: first meeting the person, then spending time together communicating, and continuing to have shared experiences.

What are some necessary ingredients for a relationship with God?

> Group members should come quickly to the realization that the same principles of building a relationship with another person (time, communication, experiences) apply to building a relationship with God.

Why We Can Have a Personal Relationship with God

1   God has chosen us.

Why is it significant that Jesus said, "I chose you?" (John 15:16)

> Christians use several terms to describe the "proper introduction" into a relationship with God: receive him, trust in Christ, born again, saved, and so on. All of these are biblical and helpful. Yet we must not overlook the fact that when we are introduced to God, he has already worked behind the scenes to facilitate that introduction. Because of his great love for us, he has sought us out. Jesus points out to his disciples that their choice was a response, not an initiative, and the same is true for us.

> For further study: John 6:44, Romans 5:6,8,10; Ephesians 1:3-4. (These verses are listed for your own preparation or for additional discussion in the group when appropriate.)

2   God wants to spend time with us.

> Once introduced, people need to spend time together. In our opening illustration we spoke of two people wanting to meet you—they wanted to go out to dinner with you. That is exactly what Jesus says he wants to do in Revelation 3:20.

What does it mean when Jesus says that he wants to eat with you? (Revelation 3:20)

> People usually go out together because they like each other and because they like to spend time with each other. They usually go out to get away from distractions (such as phone calls, other people, TV). They want to catch up with how things are going or explore issues that need in-depth conversation. This can't happen without intentionally setting aside time to be together and to communicate face-to-face.

> Two means of communication with God are through prayer and Bible study. Through prayer, we talk to God. Through the Bible, God talks to us. The term "Quiet Time" is often used to describe regular times away from distractions where we meet with God through prayer and Bible study. We will come back to expand on these points in later studies.

> For further study: Jeremiah 31:33-34, 33:3; John 14:23; 17:3.

3 God will never leave us.

> For the Christian, God is not a theological concept but a Person who walks through all of life's ups and downs with us. He calls us his children, not merely his creatures. He desires to share the journey of life with us such that no decision is made without his counsel, no plan is undertaken without his strengthening, and no trial or sorrow is faced without his comfort.

How do you respond to the promise that God will never leave us? (Hebrews 13:5)

> For further study: Isaiah 41:10; 43:1-3; Romans 8:35-39; Philippians 4:12-13

What God Has Given Us to Establish This Relationship

> Now that the group has looked at why we can have a personal relationship with God, move on to consider three gifts God has given to prove that he desires this relationship with us.

1 He gave us his Son.

What did God accomplish for us through giving his Son? (John 3:16)

> Because sin blocked any possibility of us and God relating, he had to get it out of the way. He had every right to turn his back on us the same way we had done to him. Nothing we could ever do could undo the damage done by our sin, but out of his love for us—his desire to have a relationship with us—he sent Jesus to die for

our sin and buy us back. He made a huge sacrifice for one reason: he wanted us. To him it was worth the costliest thing in the world, the blood of his Son, to have us back (and if this reunion was the most expensive thing purchased in all of history, then it's obvious we should desire it more than any of the more distracting, less expensive things in this life).

For further study: 2 Corinthians 5:18-21, Romans 8:32

2   He gave us a book.

Why is the Bible so important for our relationship with God? (Matthew 4:4)

The Bible is God's love letter, containing hundreds of pages of his thoughts about us, himself, life, and so on. God used more than forty authors, writing over 1,000 years, in three languages, on three continents. These sixty-six books had to be written, copied, protected from those who sought to destroy them, and preserved over the centuries. He brought all this together out of love for us to make sure we'd have some solid truth in the midst of so much confusion and speculation. This "library" of revelation is so filled with the wonders of the universe that we only begin to grasp its treasures in a lifetime of studying it.

For further study: Deuteronomy 29:29, Isaiah 55:10-11

3   He gave us his Spirit.

What does the Holy Spirit do for us? (John 16:13-14)

We not only come to Christ, he comes to us in the person of the Holy Spirit. It would be enough if God just associated with us—a privilege in and of itself—yet he doesn't stop at merely getting near us. He comes to indwell us at the point of our conversion. Twenty-four hours a day, seven days a week, God's Spirit has lived in us since we became believers. His own "homing device" actively works in and through us, producing Christ-like character, a hunger for spiritual growth, conviction of sin, a love for truth (the Bible), and a desire for holiness.

For further study: Ephesians 1:13-14; John 14:16-17; Romans 8:15-16.

Now that you see how much God has done to establish a relationship with you, what is your response?

If needed, refer to the six main points covered in the study. Begin with yourself if group members seem hesitant about volunteering answers. Also, be sensitive to those who may be unsure of their salvation.

**God wants a relationship with you and
has gone to great lengths to establish it.**

At the end of every study is a section called "Bottom Line." Each week you should read this summary sentence and have your group members write it down in their study guide word for word.

YOUR WALK WITH GOD

Make sure your group members understand the assignment for next week.

Bible

Schedule three times this week to get alone with God. Pick the time during the day that works best for you. Each time, read one of the first three chapters from the Gospel of John and write down one idea for application. Make a list of what you learn about Jesus from your study. Also, read over the "Benefits of a Relationship with God" in your study guide.

Prayer

Spend a few minutes praying about things that come to mind during your Bible reading. At the end of the week list two or three benefits you received from these appointments with God.

Scripture Memory

As part of the curriculum, we've included memory verses with each study. If you desire to make this discipline part of your discipleship experience, begin by memorizing this verse:

Here I am! I stand at the door and knock. If anyone hears my voice and opens the door, I will come in and eat with him, and he with me.   Revelation 3:20

Next week we will explore the topic of how to be sure you are a Christian. If you want to prepare for the discussion, think about a time you made a major decision in life (new job, major purchase, move to another city). What factors made you feel certain about your decision? You could also compare two relationships in your life—one where you knew where you stood with the person and one where you didn't. How did this knowledge affect the relationships?

The assignment at the end of each study is designed to be done during the group members' quiet time. In fact, *their homework is a quiet time.* Whatever else this small group experience does for your group members, it will help them establish a habit of regular appointments with God.

To assist members in organizing their homework, we've prepared a spiritual journey notebook called the *Walking With God Journal.* In it are instructions for doing the homework (that is, how to have a quiet time) and blank pages to write out their notes and prayers. Though purchasing the journal is not required, members may find it a useful tool as they meet with God each week.

You will also note that the homework is very basic. Please realize that you need to start simple to build success experiences. There will be more challenging assignments as the group progresses, but for now we want to begin at "square one." If your group consists of one or more mature believers, please assure them there is greater depth ahead. (You may want to challenge them to do a more elaborate study of John 1–3, using whatever Bible study methods they are already familiar with.)

PRAYER

Go around the circle having everybody pray. Complete the sentence, **Lord, I want to thank you for _____.** A word or phrase is sufficient (keep it brief). You should close after everyone has had a chance to pray.

If you sense the members of the group would be uncomfortable praying out loud at this time, simply say a closing prayer yourself.

Make sure everybody knows the time and place for the next meeting. Remind them of the need for punctuality. (Did you end the meeting on time?) Serve refreshments (if it's not too late).

Benefits of a Relationship with God

Relationships

Marriage, friendships, interaction with fellow-workers can all be renewed when you are in a right relationship with God . . . new love, new concern, new depth—not to mention all the new and different people you'll meet by participating in a local church.

Peace

The restlessness produced by unforgiven sin and purposeless activities ceases. St. Augustine in the fourth century said, "You have made us for Yourself, O God, and our hearts are restless until they find their rest in You."

Purpose

At best, life without Christ gives way to an agenda or cause; at worst, it degenerates into total self-seeking. With Christ, our lives come under the direction and guidance of an all-loving Spirit who has our best interests continuously in mind and leads us along the path of greatest significance. Any and every action we do in the Spirit has eternal value.

Fulfillment

Not just purpose and significance in life, but great satisfaction becomes the birthright of every believer. Even hard times do not diminish the sense of joy as we grow into who he created us to be.

Direction

The limited, finite perspectives on life are replaced by the counsel of an infinitely wise Advisor. All decisions, big or small, become his concerns as well as ours. Although common sense enables a Christian to choose the right path in most circumstances, God invests himself for our good and his glory in the outcome of *every* choice.

Confidence

In 1 John 4:18, the Bible says, "Perfect love drives out fear." This includes: fear of punishment (Christ already took that); fear of failure ("If God is for us, who can be against us?" [Romans 8:31]); fear of intimidation (any of our enemies are no match for the Lord); fear of loss (all that we have now belongs to

Christ—his glory in us will never be hindered by any material or circumstantial fluctuations); fear of rejection (even if all others abandon us, he will never leave us nor forsake us [see Hebrews 13:5]).

Self-Esteem

We usually do not see ourselves for who we really are; we view ourselves as what we think *others* think we are. If parents and others have constantly found fault with us, we will find fault with ourselves. No matter how objective we try to be about it, our self-esteem is to some extent at the mercy of those whom we consider important to us. When God becomes important to us, his view of us will supersede all others—and his Word abounds with promises that he loves us and that we are precious to him: We are engraved on the palms of his hands (see Isaiah 49:16).

All of these benefits and more . . . because we have a relationship with God!

How to Be Sure You're a Christian

2

OVERVIEW

The purpose of this session is to help your group members be assured of their salvation and eternal destiny.

Last week's study was devoted to the amazing truth that the God of the universe wants to have a personal relationship with us. Hopefully that truth is still making an impact on your group members. The fact that they joined your small group is probably a good indication that they want an ongoing relationship with God.

New Christians are often confused over what is promised to them as believers, and often they do not have assurance that God has forgiven them. Older believers may doubt their salvation because their Christian walk has been sporadic. Sin's power may overwhelm them at times. Still others think they're saved but do not have valid reasons for believing so. This study will comfort those who doubt and challenge those who may have false assurances of salvation. The goal for this session is to have everyone *know* where they stand with God—and know that they are secure in their relationship with him.

PRAYER

Open with a short prayer for the group as you begin this study.

Go around the circle and have each group member answer this question:

The biggest challenge I faced this week was _____.

Then have each person answer this question:

One thing I found myself appreciating this past week was _____.

Bible

Have each person share something that they learned from reading the first three chapters of the gospel of John.

Prayer

Ask: **What major concern did you pray about this week?**

Scripture Memory

Have group members either write down or recite Revelation 3:20.

No couple can build a lasting marriage if one partner is unsure of the love of the other. What if a spouse isn't even sure if the other person accepts him or her completely and doubts the other's commitment for life? A marriage with that degree of uncertainty is unstable and unhealthy. The same is true in our relationship with God. People who aren't sure of their salvation can never fully experience the blessing of their union with Christ. On the other hand, there are people who assume they will go to heaven while failing to ask what might still stand in the way. These people may live with false hope and may possibly face eternal destruction.

In this study, we will examine some of the most common misconceptions about salvation. The purpose of this session is to help you be assured of your salvation and eternal destiny.

When it comes to assurance of their salvation, people fall into three categories:

- Those who live with confidence that they have salvation
- Those who at times doubt their salvation
- Those who hope they are forgiven but lack assurance

Which category best describes you?

> Some may not have answered or may want to elaborate on the category of certainty into which they place themselves. Allow them to do so. You will probably get a mix of responses, with some people having assurance of their salvation and others not so sure. Some may even try to say that nobody can be absolutely sure. Try to keep the discussion focused on personal sharing rather than theological arguments.
>
> If appropriate for your group, ask: **If you died tonight, how certain are you that you would go to heaven?**
>
> Be sensitive to those who are unsure whether or not they are Christians.

False Assurances of Salvation

Examine the following assumptions.

I'm assured of salvation because:

"I believe there is a God."

"I'm basically a good person."

"I attend church and pray often."

"I was baptized or confirmed."

"I once prayed a prayer and asked God into my heart."

> Explore with your group members each of the "bogus tickets" people rely on to gain entrance into heaven.

1 "I believe there is a God."

How can a person believe in God and yet not have salvation?

At first, it may seem like a big step to acknowledge God's existence, especially when so many atheists do just the opposite. Some people struggle with believing in him, and so when they come to the end of the search, they assume they've "arrived" by saying, "I now believe there is a God." Yet this statement could be made by the devil! We can see this conclusion doesn't really bring us very far toward God at all.

The problem is our sin. Mere mental assent to the existence of God cannot wash away our guilt before him. It would be like acknowledging that we now believe the police officer who pulled us over for speeding really exists—but who pays the fine?

For further study: Psalm 14:1; James 2:19.

2 "I'm basically a good person."

Why is trusting in our own goodness a false basis for being included in God's kingdom?

This person assumes that because he has kept out of trouble, God has no quarrel with him. How could a fair God exclude from his presence a person with no major blemishes and many acts of charity ? But the person who relies on his or her goodness is overestimating personal righteousness and is underestimating God's holiness.

For further study: Matthew 5:48; Romans 3:23; Psalm 50:21.

3 "I attend church and pray often."

Why doesn't being religious give enough assurance of salvation?

This person assumes participation in spiritual activities means he's included in God's kingdom. This answer has again reduced salvation to something we do. And if salvation is something you earn, you never know how much is enough. What if I'm short one good deed? What if I sinned one time too many? If the standard is perfection, we all fall short.

4 "I was baptized or confirmed."

Why could a person have been baptized yet not have assurance of salvation?

This person has a little better understanding because he knows the need for something to "initiate" his relationship with God. But nowhere in the Bible does it suggest that water baptism without faith confers salvation. No matter when or how a person is baptized, faith or personal trust is essential. Even a confirmation ceremony may have been done because of parental or peer pressure without the reality behind it being present in the confirmand. As an example, a wedding band symbolizes marriage, but possessing a ring does not make one married.

Something deeper is needed.

5 "I once prayed a prayer and asked God into my heart."

How could a person invite God into his or her heart and still not have a relationship with God?

This statement may be the closest to the truth among this list of false assurances of salvation. This person knows one has to be born again. But something is still missing. Just because you prayed once or someone told you that you were a Christian doesn't mean you are. Christians are people who *have been* born again and *have been* forgiven and transformed—not just people who know they *should* be or who *want* to be. Muttering some kind of prayer many years ago doesn't mean you meant it. Jesus said people can have various responses to the gospel, but only if there is *fruit* has the real thing taken root.

For further study: Mark 4:1-20.

Genuine Assurance of Salvation

Read John 1:12.

According to this verse, what do we do?

Receive, believe in his name. Note that to "believe" means to rely on, or trust in, not merely to acknowledge as fact.

According to this verse, what does God do?

He makes us his children—he adopts us into his family.

Read John 5:24.

According to this verse, what do we do?

Hear and believe.

According to this verse, what does God do?

He gives eternal life, does not pronounce any judgment, transfers us from death to life.

Three Tests for Those Who Want to Be Sure

The Scriptures give us *evaluative tests* so we can examine our own lives for evidence that God has fulfilled his promises to us. These tests are not "things we do"; they are things he has done in us that we can see.

1 The repentance test

What does it mean for a person to repent? (Acts 3:19)

> The essence of repentance is a change of mind and heart—it literally means "to change one's mind about" or, in another phrase, "to do an about face." Ongoing conviction of sin and the desire to change indicates the Holy Spirit's work in you and is evidence of his possession of you. A saved person continues to be broken about sin; an unbeliever doesn't care or rationalizes. A saved person wants cleansing and forgiveness; an unsaved person doesn't consider guilt much of a problem. The question to answer is, "Have you turned from sin (disobedience) to God (obedience)?" Don't ask: "Have you been obedient at all times?", for nobody has! Rather find out, "Are you grieved by your disobedience—is it something you want to be free from?"

2 The presence test

What does the Holy Spirit do for a believer? (Romans 8:15-16)

> This is a subjective test, but one that is thoroughly biblical. The Holy Spirit tells us that we are his children. We feel his presence and have a peace or a calm about our spiritual condition. There's a quiet sort of confidence that we are his (not to be confused with the presumption of someone who hasn't yet seen the seriousness of his own sin). We feel we belong, even if we know we sometimes disappoint him.
>
> For further study: 2 Corinthians 13:5; John 1:12; and Revelation 3:20.

3 The evidence test

What will be true of someone who has an authentic relationship with Christ? (1 John 2:3-6)

> That person's life will be different. He or she will be living more like Christ. This is not saying true Christians never sin (see 1 John 1:8). But it is saying true believers live differently and have a verifiable behavior change—not just warm feelings. But this change takes place gradually, over time. There are degrees of spiritual maturity, so do not be discouraged if you don't feel "complete." But to experience *no* change is a warning sign that something is wrong spiritually.

If you have time, ask: **What are some of the old things that have gone and some of the new things that have come for a true Christian?** (2 Corinthians 5:17)

Some answers may include: new values and goals, character changes, new thought patterns, love for people, concern for what God thinks and feels, sacrificial living for others, a desire to break patterns of sin. Your group members may have heard at one time, "If you were arrested for being a Christian, would there be enough evidence to convict you?"

If you have time, also look at Galatians 5:22-26. Read and ask: **What attitudes and behavior characterize a true believer?**

Fruit of the spirit, harmony with God and others.

Conclusion

Read 1 John 5:11-13. What does the phrase "so that you may know" mean for us?

This could be a very significant meeting for some of your members. Be sensitive to those who may want to talk immediately following the meeting. Take the initiative to help everyone in your group settle once and for all their spiritual standing before God.

BOTTOM LINE

**God wants you to be secure
about your relationship with him.**

YOUR WALK WITH GOD

Central to the values behind the *Walking With God Series* is the belief that "homework" should not compete with a believer's regular appointments with God. Therefore, in this curriculum, a person's walk with God *is* the homework. Considering the pace of modern life, we thought it impractical for the average person to complete lengthy assingments *and* have quiet times. This material was designed to help you with the minimum requirements we considered necessary to maintain a vital connection with God.

To help you follow the regular assignments in this series, we have prepared the *Walking With God Journal*. In addition to providing pages for writing out the assignments, the journal contains practical advice on Bible study, prayer, and memorization. You'll also find suggestions for keeping quiet times fresh and creative tips on how to apply Bible knowledge to your life.

Bible

Make three appointments with God. Read 1 John chapters 1–2 and list as many reasons as possible for a person to know that he or she is a Christian. Also read "What Is God Like?"

Prayer

Pray over any concerns that come to mind. Also, identify something for which you can be thankful.

Scripture Memory

I write these things to you who believe in the name of the Son of God so that you may know that you have eternal life.   1 John 5:13

Next time we will begin the first of two lessons on personal Bible study. If you want to prepare for the study, think about different ways that you can get teachings of the Bible into your life. Then consider why the Bible is important and what it does for us.

PRAYER

Lead the group in a closing prayer.

What Is God Like?

Most people think they know the answer to that question. It wouldn't even occur to them that they might not have an accurate picture of God. "Everybody knows what God is like! He's, uh, well he's . . ." What follows is a mishmash of ideas heard from parents and teachers over the years, uncritically examined but firmly believed. At an even deeper level, what people *feel* toward God flows out of their life experiences—and is equally subjective and untested.

"My grandma talked about God, and she was very nice to me—I guess I see God like her."

"I grew up in a very strict home with lots of rules—pretty much like God treats me now."

"Most ministers say God loves me—I guess he's like that."

"Most ministers say God is really mad at me—I guess he's like that."

Let's begin with this assumption: some of our perspectives of God are wrong. We've seen too much, been hurt too much, been confused too much to assert we've got an accurate picture of God in every area. Somehow we got some misinformation—every one of us. So we'll either have to take deliberate steps to reeducate ourselves about what he's like, or our view of him will continue out of focus . . . and will probably get worse with time.

Where do we begin to get an accurate picture? A good place to start is with what God has done—by seeing his acts we can get a picture of the One responsible. Just as art tells us something about the artist, or a person's work tells us about his or her abilities and interests, what God has created tells us about what he, the Creator, is like. As we look at creation—nature, the world, the stars and galaxies—one undeniable conclusion emerges: the One responsible for all this must be powerful beyond comparison. From the tiniest single-cell amoeba to entire distant galaxies racing at near the speed of light, from an intricately complex snowflake to a sunset that sends amber blasts of color across the expansive sky, God's handiwork is so evident that you actively have to suppress what you see and feel in order to ignore him.

Yet the Bible tells us that's exactly what we do (Romans 1:18-20). That inner sense of his majesty—clearly evident in the cosmos—is squelched. We hear the Voice . . . and ignore it. And so while we all carry around some sense of his grandeur, we've modified and molded our image of him until the gap between who we perceive him to be and who he really is becomes uncrossable. Sin—our deliberate attempts to expel him from the throne of the universe as well as our passive indifference to his rule—not only messes up our lives, it messes up our view of God.

But our condition is not hopeless. God doesn't just *do*—he *speaks*. He talks to us. He sends messages. He tells us the truth through prophets and leaders. The Bible is the written record of his love. We learn from this book things we couldn't know otherwise.

For one thing, we learn that the sense of awe we get from his creation needs to be cultivated and expanded. Every notion we have of his power is true—and then some. But we learn also that his power is restrained. He isn't an angry father about to blow his cool. He's a loving Father desiring to be close. In the earliest parts of the Bible we see God calling out a single man, Abraham, for a special purpose: to make a nation that would represent him to the world. That group of people was intended to be a tangible picture of his love, power, justice, and holiness. They'd be different from the rest of the world—because he is different. They'd be holy—because he is holy. They'd show compassion—because he is compassionate. They'd avoid sin—because he has no sin. They'd be blessed—because it's his nature to bless. Next to the picture of God painted in creation would be this picture painted through a unique group of people. He would talk to them, and talk *through* them.

But God didn't just *do* and didn't just *speak*. He *became*. His work ordered the nothingness and made it a world for all to see. His word came to the prophets and made a book for all to read. The pinnacle of his communication was his Word coming to dwell among us in Jesus for all to receive. We *see* his handiwork; we *read* his book; we *meet* his Son. Jesus is the ultimate picture of God—the work and Word of God incarnate. What he does, God does. What he loves, God loves. What he hates, God hates. What he says, God says. How he acts, God acts. Look no further for clarification of what God is like: the only begotten Son has fully explained him (John 1:18). He showed God's awesome power by stilling the storm, healing the sick, and raising the dead—creation was subject to him. He showed God's desire to speak to us by unsurpassed teaching—truth was fully represented by him. And he lived out God's compassion without compromising his righteousness—God's nature was completely embodied in him. Nowhere was this more forcefully demonstrated than through his death on our behalf. By hating sin, God shows justice. By forgiving sin, he shows mercy. But by *being the payment* for that sin himself, he shows matchless, marvelous, magnificent grace.

This, then, is what God is like. Theologians have come up with words that summarize these qualities, or "attributes," as they're known. Once we get past the somewhat formal feel of these terms, they can be useful tools to encapsulate what we know about God. Here's a list of the main attributes.

What God Is — Ways We Can' t Be Like Him

Omnipresent: God is always near; no place is farther from him than any other place; he is not limited to any spatial dimensions.

Omnipotent: God can do anything that doesn't violate his nature; he's all-powerful; nothing is impossible for him; his power is unlimited and unrestricted except by his own choice.

Omniscient: God knows everything; nothing is hidden; nothing goes unnoticed; no situation is beyond his ability to grasp; all mysteries are clear to him; no one can tell him something he doesn't already know.

Sovereign: God is the ultimate ruler of the universe; no one is greater in authority or power than he; no sin or disobedience can thwart the purposes he desires to bring to pass.

Eternal: God has always been; he will always be; he had no beginning; he'll have no end; he is the creator of time; he is not subject to time but rules over it.

Immutable: God doesn't change; he isn't getting better; his beauty can't be diminished; he doesn't grow or increase; he's perfect the way he is, and we can rest assured he will continue that way.

Infinite: God is unlimited; whatever he is, he is to an infinite degree; you can't measure any part of him or his attributes; he is inexhaustible in every aspect of his being.

Who God Is — Ways We Should Imitate Him

Holy: God is pure; he's without fault; he can't be compared to anyone or anything because he's so different from all we've known or experienced.

Wise: God uses his knowledge skillfully; he makes sense; he is no fool; his counsel can be trusted.

Good: God has no evil and can do no evil; he works for the benefit of his creatures; he can be trusted with our well-being.

Just: God is fair; he doesn't tolerate unrighteousness; he will make sure every wrong will be made right; he is impartial.

Loving: Sacrifice is in God's very nature; he cares; he gives; he serves; he works to bring about what we need; he's compassionate; he's sensitive; he chooses to let us matter to him.

We can come up with many other words that describe him as well: merciful, kind, pure, righteous, patient, faithful, trustworthy, generous, awesome, majestic, etc. These qualities will all be, to some degree, aspects of the main attributes we've listed. The more you get to know the Bible, the more you'll discover the manifold descriptions of his nature. Look for new ways of describing him. Worship him for the many and varied facets of his being. Learn who he really is, so you can gradually replace the shadows in your mind with the substance of his true nature.

What is God like? Maybe this song says it best: "Jesus loves me this I know, for the Bible tells me so . . ."

God's Word to You

3

OVERVIEW

The purpose of this study is to help your group understand the value of personal Bible study.

Anyone can rattle off reasons for Bible reading and studying. But this session will be a success if you can persuade your group members that *their* spiritual fulfillment depends upon regular study of the Scriptures. Strive to have the group members be acutely aware of the many benefits of God's Word. What they do—this week and in the weeks and months ahead—will determine if the content of this study has sunk in, because the emphasis of this study is transformation, not just information. This is the first of two lessons on Bible study.

PRAYER

Open the meeting with prayer.

OPENER

You may want to have the group answer the following questions seriously or humorously. Try to sense if group members need a moment of self-disclosure and support or if they just need a good laugh.

The most significant thing that happened in my life this week was _____.

If I could do one thing over this past week, I would change _____.

Bible

Ask your group members to share what they learned about assurance of salvation from 1 John 1–2.

Prayer

Ask: **What were you thankful for?**

Scripture Memory

To review the Scripture memory assignment, have them recite 1 John 5:13.

Think back to a time when you received a letter from a close friend or a special someone who was away on summer vacation or for the school year. How did you feel when you received the envelope? How long did you wait to read the letter inside?

It is puzzling, then, to consider that many Christians are interested in knowing what God is saying to them yet neglect to read the letters and messages God has prepared for them. The Bible is God's love letter to all those who trust in Christ. It makes sense, then, that we should learn all we can about God's Word, for it is his primary means of speaking to us. The purpose of this meeting is to help you understand the value of personal Bible study.

Five Ways We Grasp God's Word

©1976 by The Navigators and used by permission

1 Hear (Romans 10:17)

What are some ways to hear God's Word?

2 Read (Revelation 1:3)

In what forms can you read God's Word?

3 Study (Acts 17:11)

What are some ways to study God's Word?

4 Memorize (Psalm 119:11)

What might be the benefits of memorizing God's Word?

5 Meditate (Psalm 1:2-3)

What does it mean to meditate on God's Word?

If you were to pick up the Bible with only two fingers, you wouldn't have much control over it. But if you grasp the Bible firmly with all five fingers, then you would have a better grip. In your spiritual pilgrimage, try to move down the list until all of these methods help you "firmly hold onto God's truth."

What Will God's Word Do for Me?

1   It will help me grow spiritually. (1 Peter 2:2)

What parallels can you see between an infant and its food and a Christian and the Bible?

A hungry baby is a healthy baby—a spiritually hungry Christian is a spiritually healthy Christian. Spiritual birth produces life, but that life cannot be sustained without spiritual nourishment. That food is found in the Bible. As Jesus said "Man does not live on bread alone, but on every word that comes from the mouth of God."(Matthew 4:4). A baby craves its mother's milk, and we must crave our heavenly parent's food. And just as the baby enjoys that food when given, so should we enjoy the Word that nourishes us.

2   It will help me be honest with myself. (Hebrews 4:12)

How does it feel to be "penetrated" by God's truth?

The Word of God shines as a searchlight on our dark regions of self-deception. It shows us who we are and reveals our true nature. As we read it, it convicts us of sins we weren't even aware of. We may be able to keep others from looking deep inside us, but God's Word gets to the very core of our being, dividing soul and spirit. It even exposes the selfish motives behind many of our actions. Without the "active" Word showing us our corrupt nature, we might have fooled ourselves into believing in our own goodness. This "double-edged sword" sweeps in all directions, performing its cutting, revealing, and exposing work. No other book on earth has such power to make us honest with ourselves.

3   It equips me for good work. (2 Timothy 3:16-17)

Who is the author of the Bible?

God didn't just get human authors excited and then let them write whatever they wanted. He worked through them in a remarkable way so that what they wrote were God's words. All Scripture is God-breathed—full of power and life. The result is that we are equipped for every good work. This means we have the tools we need for serving God.

What are the Scriptures good for in the life of the Christian?

When we learned to drive, we started going to classes (teaching). Then we got behind the wheel and ran over a curb on our first turn. After the instructor yelled at us (rebuking), he showed us how to get off the sidewalk and back onto the road (correcting). Then he went through the right way to judge and make a turn so that from then on we could do it properly (training).

4 It renews my mind. (Romans 12:1-2)

In what ways do you think God's Word could renew your mind?

> God calls us to reprogram our minds according to his truths. Through the five ways of grasping God's Word, we purify and redirect our thoughts and affections. This process is not just a matter of replacing bad thoughts with good thoughts, or negative ideas with positive ones—it is making a habit of relying on God's perspective rather than our own. Gradually, we develop an unconscious biblical response to life situations as our minds are renewed. We will do God's will without even thinking when we constantly renew our minds according to his Word.

5 It helps me be successful in life. (Joshua 1:8)

What is your view of success?

> We can rejoice that promises such as these assure us of great blessing that comes from meditating on and obeying God's law. Success, of course, has to be carefully defined—it is certainly not the mere presence of wealth or the absence of hardships. Neither our Lord nor any other biblical character lived a prosperous, trouble-free existence at all times. Yet our blessings are not limited to spiritual blessings, either. A Christian with a balanced perspective realizes that while at all times we are rich spiritually, often values taught in Scripture (such as self-discipline and the value of human labor) may actually improve our material position—often, but not always.

Additional Benefits

> Here are some additional passages to cover with your group if desired or if extra time is available.

6 It puts truth at my fingertips. (2 Timothy 2:15)

What are some specific parallels between a workman and his tools and the Christian and his Bible?

> The Bible is called the Word of Truth. Do you want truth in your life? Truth about God? About your reason for living? About what you're really like, and about what God really thinks about you? About what the future holds? All this and more is available to those who diligently study God's Word.

7 It protects us from attack. (Ephesians 6:17)

How does the way a soldier uses a sword compare with how a Christian can use the Word?

Of all the armor mentioned in this passage, the sword—the Word—is the only *offensive* weapon. The Bible is not only capable of helping us find security, but also of equipping us to destroy that which threatens our security. Its truths help us both grow strong spiritually within and resist the temptations which come from outside us. Jesus turned aside Satan's temptations not with brute force or even prayer alone, but with quotations from God's Word directed specifically and aggressively against the enemy.

8   It influences others. (Deuteronomy 6:6-7)

How does the Bible help you to have a spiritual influence on your family or others?

One of the chief goals of parenting is living out and teaching godly values to our children. As we look around us, there are many who are not related to us who also need this same influence of godliness. It is interesting to note that this passage commands sharing these values not in the classroom or in church, but in the day-to-day routines of life. God's Word should saturate us; then we can saturate others with it.

BOTTOM LINE

**Give God every opportunity to speak to
you personally through his Word.**

YOUR WALK WITH GOD

Bible

Read 1 John 3 the first day, 1 John 4 the second day, and 1 John 5 the third day. Make a list of all the truths in these chapters that have to do with love (love to others, love to God, love from God, and so on).

Prayer

Pray for another person this week.

Scripture Memory

All Scripture is God-breathed and is useful for teaching, rebuking, correcting and training in righteousness, so that the man of God may be thoroughly equipped for every good work.   2 Timothy 3:16-17

Next time we will take a closer look at the difference between *reading* the Bible and *studying* the Bible. If you want to prepare, think back to a time when you had to study a book for a test. In what ways was that experience different from simply reading the material for pleasure?

PRAYER

Close with a prayer or ask someone in the group to do so.

God's Word in You

4

OVERVIEW

This session will help your group learn how to use an inductive method to study the Bible.

Most busy people need a method of Bible study that conveys spiritual truths in a concise manner. Those who may be more mature in the faith, or have more time, can be coaxed into embarking on in-depth study programs that make use of commentaries, Bible dictionaries, and other reference tools. But while there will always be a few hardy souls who can handle more work, this inductive Bible study method is intended for the average person who—like most of us—has a full schedule.

PRAYER

You or a group member should open the meeting with prayer.

OPENER

Here are some discussion starters that emphasize thanksgiving. You may want to try a different theme or just make up some fun statements for a change.

Two experiences that I'm thankful I had this last year are _____ and _____.

The one thing I'm most thankful for about my spouse (or close friend) is _____.

Bible

Ask group members to share the truths they came up with about love in their Bible reading (1 John 3—5). Make sure you have a list of your own to share.

If some of your people didn't do the assignment, follow through with a phone call to see what changes they can make so that they can complete their assignment. Remember, you are trying to build accountability.

Prayer

Ask how they did this week praying for another person. If it is appropriate to share, ask them who or what they prayed for.

Scripture Memory

Have the group members write down or recite 2 Timothy 3:16-17.

PURPOSE

The difference between Bible reading and Bible study is often a pencil. When we write things down, we achieve greater clarity and deeper understanding, making lessons learned easier to integrate into life. In the same way that we might find a rare nugget of gold lying on the ground, we can happen upon some valuable truths by simply browsing through the pages of Scripture. But to find a richer vein of gold, we have to go beneath the surface—and this discovery requires study.

While some may enjoy study for its own sake, the purpose of this lesson is to show how Bible study allows us to uncover truths that can transform our character. This study will help you learn how to use an inductive method to study the Bible.

As a review of the last meeting, ask group members to list from memory the five ways to grasp God's Word:

Hear

Read

Study

Memorize

Meditate

Tell them this lesson will take an in-depth look at the third way—study—to grasp God's Word.

Four Approaches to Personal Bible Study

Despite their good intentions, many Christians develop problems that hinder effective personal Bible study. The first three groups characterize typical problems while the fourth gives us the correct approach.

1   The Sitters

These people do not do personal Bible study at all. They would rather "sit at the feet" of someone who will explain the Bible to them.

What are the sitters missing by not studying the Bible themselves?

They reap the benefits of other people's study, but never enjoy the process of discovery on their own. They will "sit under" someone's teaching readily enough, but they won't search the Scriptures for themselves. Unfortunately, many Christians are in this camp and are really missing out. Although there is great value in learning from others who diligently study God's Word, there is no replacement for direct input from God through personal Bible study.

2   The Skimmers

These people go beyond the sitters and actually read God's Word themselves. They may also regularly read some kind of daily devotional book.

What do the skimmers miss by not going deeper into the Word?

They are definitely better off than those who don't read at all, and this is a great place to start because of the individual interaction with the Scriptures. However, the Bible is a book that needs to be studied as well as read. Many of its truths cannot be grasped without more detailed analysis. The people in this camp need to be applauded for their willingness to go beyond passive learning, but they need to be encouraged to go deeper.

3 The Scholars

This group of people, though small in number, is very much at home when studying the Bible in a scholarly manner, assisted by commentaries, Bible dictionaries, and other reference tools.

Why might the "scholars" find that their methods do not necessarily produce spiritual growth?

> Although the "scholars" should be praised for their hard work and appetite for biblical knowledge, these people need to be careful, lest they become dependent on commentaries and subtly begin to displace the authority of God's Word with the authority of some of their favorite authors. They can develop into book-oriented "sitters." Like the sitters, they may get truth only second-hand or third-hand instead of wrestling with the text themselves. Also, the scholars may have a tendency to reduce their learning to head knowledge, and thus Bible study becomes detached from spiritual growth and personal application.

4 The Students

These people are like the person that Paul describes in 2 Timothy 2:15. This is the category your group members should want to be in.

Read 2 Timothy 2:15. What qualities does the "workman" Paul describes possess?

> The people Paul describes are on a lifetime quest to know and live God's Word. Like them, we should study the Bible seriously (in a way that has reasonable time commitments with maximum personal benefits). A key method to employ is called inductive Bible study.

A Five-Step Inductive Bible Study Method

Step 1: Background

What kind of questions might you ask to learn more about the background of any book or passage that you are studying?

The questions you ask are those of a good reporter:

- Who wrote the book (letter)?
- To whom was it written?

- What were the circumstances surrounding its writing?

- Why was it written?

- What main themes come through?

Any commentary, Bible dictionary, or study Bible contains this information. Books like these are a lifetime investment in your spiritual growth and are well worth owning.

Once you know the answer to these background questions, your study will come alive and the characters will seem more real. This also guards against erroneous interpretations because you can better discern the intent of the biblical author.

Step 2: Read

Why is it a good idea to read a whole book of the Bible completely through before analyzing its parts?

The primary benefit of this approach is that it allows you to grasp the book's broader themes and understand particular passages in context. Try using several translations. After three or four readings, write out a sentence summary of the author's overall message and objective. Underline some of the key verses that support that message.

With shorter books (like 1 John), one sitting is enough to read the whole book. With larger books (Gospels, Psalms, Proverbs, 1 or 2 Corinthians, and others) you will need to divide the book into major sections.

Step 3: Observe

How do you determine what a passage of Scripture is saying?

The key to accurate observations is to look for the original intent of the person who wrote the book. After several cursory readings, ask yourself *What is the author saying to his audience?* Divide the book into sections and simply write down in your own words the main points of each section. If it is a longer book, you can go back and expand on your observations during a second or third time through.

Note: Some of your group members may comment that we shouldn't confuse observation with interpretation, and they are right. Technically, we must separate the two, though for our purposes here we have not emphasized that distinction in the notes they write out. After observing what the passage is saying, they need to decide what it means—in other words, they need to *interpret* the passage. We should keep in mind, however, that jumping to an interpretation without careful observation easily leads to *mis*interpretation. A good interpretation is supported by the passage (and often by other passages); while a poor interpretation reflects the unsupported personal bias of the observer. As they write out their observations, make sure they note accurately only what the Scripture says. When studying difficult passages, they may want to consult a commentary or two to check their findings with what others have observed.

Step 4: Apply

How do you apply what you learn to your daily life?

Once careful observations have been made, the next step is to meditate prayerfully on the text and make specific, personal applications. These applications can relate to any part of your life: home, family, work, church, friends, money, and so on. When you ask God, "What do you want me to do now based on this passage, Lord?", you can be confident it is a prayer he is *very* interested in answering (see James 1:22; Isaiah 66:2; Hebrews 4:2)

Here are examples of application questions that you can use:

Is there a promise to claim?

> (Hebrews 13:5)

Is there a command to obey?

> (Ephesians 5:21)

Is there sin to confess?

> (1 Corinthians 6:1-20)

Is there an example to follow?

> (1 Thessalonians 2:5)

Is there a behavior to change?

> (Ephesians 4:25-32)

Is there an encouragement to receive?

> (Philippians 4:13)

Is there an insight to gain?

> (Romans 8:28)

Is there an issue to pray about?

> (1 Timothy 2:3-4)

Is there a reason to worship God?

> (Romans 11:33-36)

Though it is important to have specific applications, allow for times when truths deeply impress and encourage your spirit. Sometimes, simply valuing and being encouraged by God's promises is the most helpful application.

Step 5: Memorize

Why is memorization important for personal Bible study?

Memorization produces the most far-reaching and long-lasting effects of Bible study. By committing to memory portions of Scripture, you will have readily available truths that the Holy Spirit can help you recall in times of need. An added benefit is that your mind becomes occupied with positive and enriching thoughts. Choose key verses from the book you're studying that encapsulate truths worth remembering. Hide those truths in your heart through memorization (see Psalm 119:11).

Now that your group member have these steps in mind, note that a convenient way to remember them is the acronym:

BROAM
Background, Read, Observe, Apply, Memorize

The two key steps in this process are *observing* and *applying*. As you will see, these are at the heart of the following weekly homework assignments.

Practice: Observe and Apply

Turn to James 1:2-4 to see how this inductive method works on an actual portion of Scripture. This abbreviated study will emphasize two of the five steps—*observation* and *application*—because you will spend most of your time doing these steps during your appointments with God.

Observation: "What does it say?"	Application: "What should I do?"

Observation: "What does it say?"

Ask the group members to list their observations—here are some ideas for further discussion:

- Be joyful when trials come—they can be useful for producing some greater good in our lives.

- Know that when you faith is tested, you grow in endurance.

- The result of endurance is a faith that lacks nothing.

- God's hands aren't tied when we go through hard times—he is able to work even in our hardship.

- Growing is more important than comfort. We can handle life with God's help.

Application: "What should I do?"

Again, ask for group ideas from James 1:2-4 first. Here are some additional suggestions:

- Think of a trial you are going through or one you can look back on—show your "joy" regarding this by thanking God, right now, that he is (was) working in your life. This will probably not be easy, so you will need to pray for strength for this to occur.

- Call or write a note to someone going through a trial. Encourage them (of course, don't be glib about it—"weep with those who weep" may be more appropriate), let them know you're praying, and pray three times a week for their joy and endurance.

If you would prefer, here are some other passages you may want to go through instead of (or, time permitting, in addition to) James 1:2-4:

- 1 John 1:5-10 (forgiveness)

- Jude 17-23 (false Christians)

- 1 Peter 2:13-17 (our attitudes toward civil authority)

- Hebrews 4:14-16 (help in our weakness)

- Mark 12:28-34 (the greatest commandment)

> **Wisdom from God is available to those who are
> lifetime students of the Bible.**

YOUR WALK WITH GOD

Take a few moments to make sure everyone in your group is clear on what they are to do before next week.

Bible

Study James 1 on three different occasions and list observations and applications. You may either study the whole chapter three times (perhaps using a different version each time) or read one-third of the chapter each time so the assignment is completed by the next study. Make one personal application for each day of study. Attempt to make your applications as specific as possible.

Prayer

In addition to your own personal concerns, pray this week for a particular ministry within your church.

Scripture Memory

Review verses you have learned so far: Revelation 3:20; 1 John 5:13; 2 Timothy 3:16-17.

In the next study we will learn more about the importance of memorizing Scripture. To prepare, try to recall the last time you had to memorize something for an important event. What helped you remember the information most effectively?

PRAYER

The leader or group member should close the meeting in prayer.

Taking God's Word to Heart

This session will help your group understand the importance and benefits of memorizing Scripture.

The human brain is a marvelous creation. Even considering the amazing achievements of modern computers, the brain is matchless in its ability to store and retrieve information. Using some of that memory capacity for storing Scripture is a discipline many have found beneficial. And it is one that deserves the consideration of everyone in your group.

One of the first objections people raise on the matter of memorizing Scripture comes as an expression of inability: "But you don't understand, I *can't* memorize." But where is that *can't* coming from? When we stop and think about it, we may be simply making excuses. No one can deny that memorization requires effort. But it is *possible.* Clearly, it is an effort that won't be wasted. Remind the reluctant ones that God has equipped them with a wonderful brain that they are to use to enjoy his revealed Word. By trusting God for help, Scripture memorization will be within the reach of everyone in the group.

PRAYER

Open the meeting with prayer.

Have each person complete these statements:

On my way over here for our meeting I spent most of my time thinking (or talking) about _____.

Lately during idle moments, my mind seems to drift back predictably to _____.

REVIEW

Bible

Have each person share their favorite observation and application from James 1:1-27.

Prayer

Have each person tell about the particular church ministry they prayed for. If you have time, ask them why they chose the ministry they did and what they prayed for?

Scripture Memory

Have the group recite all verses learned up through the last study.

PURPOSE

Imagine that you are a carpenter starting the first day at a new work site. As you begin your first task, you remember that all your tools are at home in your basement! You drive back home, get your hammer, and return to work. The same happens when you need a saw. Everyone else on the job is frustrated by the slowdown of having to wait for you. This pattern continues the rest of the day—every time you need a tool, you have to go home and get it. The situation gets worse later in the day when you cut your hand badly. The ambulance arrives within minutes, but the paramedics have to return to the hospital to get *their* equipment. They promise to get back to you as soon as they can.

A bad dream, right? This whole scene seems intolerable because of one obvious oversight: those who need their tools don't have them when and where they need them.

Yet many Christians approach their daily activities with a similar unpreparedness. They often neglect to carry with them the truths and promises of God's Word. Because it isn't always practical to flip to the Bible when faced with a difficult situation, Christians need more than just familiarity with the Scriptures—they need knowledge of what God says *on the spot and at the moment.* And one of the best ways to have his Word readily accessible is through memorization. This study will help you understand the importance and benefits of memorizing Scripture.

STUDY

Read Luke 4:1-13. What do you observe about Jesus' responses to the devil?

> The obvious pattern in Jesus' answers was that he quoted Scripture. He certainly didn't have an Old Testament handy at the moment, so he had to draw on passages that had been committed to memory. We might think that because of Jesus' greater power or purity, he could fight Satan more easily than we can. Yet his successful resistance required the ready availability of God's Word.

In what kinds of situations might having passages of Scripture committed to memory be helpful to you?

Great Reasons to Memorize Scripture

> Next, cover the following list of benefits that come from memorizing Scripture. Allow group members to share occasions where they have experienced each benefit.

In what way can memorizing Scripture . . .

1. Purify your thoughts? (Philippians 4:8)

> Rather than merely suppressing evil thoughts, you can replace them with portions of Scripture.

2. Increase your effectiveness in prayer? (John 15:7)

Memorization can help you remain (or abide) in Christ, and thus your requests will be more in accordance with his will.

3. Be useful in witnessing? (Acts 8:35-36)

Christians can have a great impact on other people when they know the issues that confront nonbelievers and have a sure command of Scripture as it relates to those areas.

4. Help you meditate? (see Psalm 119:97)

When you want to spend some time thinking about God or praising him, dwelling on a verse that describes an attribute of God is a wonderful way to start.

5. Enrich your Bible study? (2 Timothy 3:16)

Scripture committed to memory is a handy cross-reference tool. It is also more readily available to apply as you go through your daily routine.

6. Enhance your counseling or teaching? (Proverbs 15:23)

At the appropriate time, God's Word can be a powerful agent for healing, teaching, or advising.

7. Provide guidance for decisions? (Psalm 119:24)

Many verses of the Bible, when committed to memory, can help to keep us on the right path as we go through our day.

8. Provide encouragement when you're feeling down? (Romans 15:4)

Because tough times will always be with us, it's useful to keep the Scriptures with us at all times, too.

9. Strengthen you when tempted? (Psalm 37:31)

Using Scripture is one way to resist the devil and the power of our own evil desires.

10. Increase your faith? (Romans 10:17)

The more we know of God, the more we will be able to trust him.

Helps for Memorization

Now take a few moments to help your group members with some practical tips for memorization. These steps do not require much discussion but should be noted as you wrap up this study.

What do you see as the value of each of the following steps?

1 Focus on the benefit

Your conviction that God's Word is indispensable to your Christian life will provide motivation for learning.

2 Know the meaning

First understand what you want to remember. Learn it a phrase at a time and let the meaning come through.

3 Use your imagination

Try to "see" the verse in your mind.

4 Don't forget to review

By going back through previously learned verses, you will recall them for years to come.

5 Involve others

Practice memorization with fellow believers. You can work together, review together, and share the benefits together.

At this point you can call attention to the Scripture memory portions of the assignments for each study. Agreeing together to do these as a group and taking the time to review can be a great way to implement the steps you've just discussed. You may also want to share the following caveat: Scripture memory can turn into a sort of badge of spiritual achievement. Jesus warned against such hypocritical behavior (Matthew 23:5). If you take on this discipline, be aware this potential abuse.

Meditation and Memorization

What does it mean to meditate on God's Word?

To meditate simply means to mull over, consider, rethink, or ruminate on something. And what is more worthy of meditation than God's Word? One of the benefits of Scripture memory is the ease with which you can have something to meditate on—if you've memorized portions of the Bible, they are readily available to ponder.

Note: In eastern religions, the practice of meditation is quite different than that of meditating on Scripture. The goal of eastern meditation is to empty one's mind of cognitive activity and achieve an altered state of consciousness. Christian meditation, on the other hand, requires cognitive activity centered on objective truth, not the empty repetition of mantra (see Matthew 6:7). Eastern meditation connects a person to his inner self (at least, it is claimed); Christian meditation on Scripture connects a person to God.

Read Psalm 119:97. When is the best time of the day for meditation?

> Meditation is a lifestyle, not simply an activity. It is parallel to "praying without ceasing" (1 Thessalonians 5:17)

Note: For additional insights on memorizing Scripture, see Bob Siefert, "You Can Memorize Scripture," in *Discipleship Journal* (Issue 9, 1982), p. 36, and Francis Cosgrove, *The Essentials of Discipleship* (Colorado Springs: NavPress, 1980).

BOTTOM LINE

**Memorizing Scripture enables us
to take God's Word to heart.**

YOUR WALK WITH GOD

Bible

Read James 2 in each of your three appointments with God this week. List observations and at least one application for each time of Bible study.

Prayer

Pray that God will help you memorize his Word and internalize it so that you are better able to do what the Bible says (James 1:22).

Scripture Memory

I have hidden your word in my heart that I might not sin against you.   Psalm 119:11

In the next study we will begin to explore the topic of prayer. To prepare, think about a time that you prayed for something specific. What happened or didn't happen as a result of your prayer? What principles about prayer would you give to a new believer?

PRAYER

Close with a prayer or ask someone in the group to do so.

Ground Rules for Prayer

OVERVIEW

This study will help your group understand how God answers prayer.

Because prayer is simply talking with God, no practice should be easier or more natural. Yet, in reality, many believers find prayer to be very difficult. Your group members' experience and maturity regarding this discipline will be diverse. Some will have more experience. For others, it will be a new challenge. Because prayer is one of the most important disciplines in the believer's life, this study is vital for your group members. Therefore, a little extra prayer about this study on prayer would be in order!

PRAYER

The leader or a designated group member should open the meeting with prayer. In future weeks, as members become more comfortable with prayer, ask different individuals to open.

OPENER

Ask group members to think back to a recent time when somebody did something that they regard as one of their pet peeves. How did they react?

Bible

Ask your group members to share their favorite observation and application from James 2:1-26.

Prayer

Have them share what they prayed about regarding memorization of the Word.

Scripture Memory

Have group members recite Psalm 119:11.

Would you prefer reading a book by candlelight or by a bright overhead light? If you're like most people, you would choose the overhead light. Although candlelight has a certain beauty about it, it's quite limited in the amount of light it can give. Besides, a gust of wind could blow it out or someone could easily extinguish it. To accomplish any amount of reading without severe eyestrain, we need the overhead light to illuminate the book's pages. And to get this light, we must use a switch.

In the spiritual realm, prayer is the switch that allows the power of the Holy Spirit to illuminate our lives. Many Christians live their lives guided only by their own natural light, their own wisdom and power. But by using the switch of prayer, the Holy Spirit intercedes and causes the Father's light to bathe our lives. Prayer is the difference—the power is there already. It just has to be "switched on." This study will help you understand how God answers prayer. We will explore four principles of prayer from the Bible and the four kinds of answers that God gives.

Four Principles of Prayer

1   The Holy Spirit helps us to know what and how to pray (Romans 8:26)

In what ways are we weak when it comes to prayer?

Describe a time when you were frustrated with not knowing how to pray.

> The answer to these frustrations is found in the latter part of Romans 8:26.

2   The Holy Spirit intercedes on our behalf (Romans 8:26)

What do you think are some of the personal benefits of having the Holy Spirit pray for you?

> He prays for needs that we cannot express fully.

> Note: Some may wonder if it's Jesus or the Holy Spirit who is supposed to intercede for us. According to Romans 8:34, Jesus also intercedes for us.

> Note: Some in your group may ask why the Spirit "groans." Just as creation groans (8:22) and we groan (8:23), the Holy Spirit groans as he pleads for us. The sincerity and depth of his feelings for us transcends description. Thus, he is said to have groanings "that words cannot express."

3   God hears our hearts in prayer more than our words (Romans 8:27)

What comfort is there in knowing that God searches our hearts?

> It reminds us that God is intimately concerned with our well-being.

Read Matthew 6:5-8. What "errors" in prayer does Jesus mention?

> Many pray with great eloquence, but their prayers don't seem to go higher than the ceiling. Others stumble and struggle, but because their hearts are full, the Lord hears those requests. The issue in effective prayer is not propriety but sincerity.

4   Prayer is always answered (Romans 8:28-29)

In what ways might God be at work even when he doesn't give an immediate "yes" to our prayers?

God is always working for our good, and this good is being conformed to Christ. So even when some of our prayers are answered negatively, God is working to conform us to the image of his Son.

Four Ways God Answers Prayer

1   No—Your request is wrong (Matthew 26:36-39)

What are some examples of prayer requests you know God would say "no" to?

Even Jesus received a "no" to his request to not have to go to the cross. Some requests don't fulfill God's larger purposes, and so he turns us down. Of course, some requests are morally wrong, such as "Lord, help me to steal this car" or, "Lord, is it OK if I sleep with my girlfriend?" Obviously, God would say no to those requests, too!

For further study: 2 Samuel 12:15-23.

2   Slow—Your timing is wrong (John 11:1-6)

What are some examples of prayer requests that God might say "slow" to?

The wrong timing here is not necessarily a moral fault. The wrongness is in our preconceived idea of when God should act. It's OK to ask now, but sometimes we have to wait for the answer.

For further study: Genesis 15:2-6; 21:2

3   Grow—Your spiritual condition is wrong (James 4:2-3)

In what ways might God ask you to grow before he gives you a "yes" to a prayer?

There are cases where wrong motives (though not necessarily a wrong request) hinder response to a prayer.

For further study: Numbers 14:26-45, 1 Peter 3:7

4   Go—Your request, timing, and spiritual condition are OK (Acts 12:5-17)

What are some of your prayers that God has answered with a "yes"?

Note that in Acts 12:15, the believers had trouble believing God had answered their request!

For further study: 1 Kings 18:36-39; James 5:17-18

What will it take for you to become a person who prays more?

If we don't pray:

God loses—because he enjoys us and likes to hear from us

We lose—because we live without the full amount of light God desires to give.

BOTTOM LINE

Pray, because God hears and answers every prayer.

YOUR WALK WITH GOD

Bible

Keep three appointments with God, studying James 3:1-18. Note observations and applications. Also, reread the Scripture passages from the section "Four Ways God Answers Prayer."

Prayer

Pray about those areas in your life where you need God's wisdom and strength.

Scripture Memory

Do not be anxious about anything, but in everything, by prayer and petition, with thanksgiving, present your requests to God. And the peace of God, which transcends all understanding, will guard your hearts and your minds in Christ Jesus. Philippians 4:6-7

We will learn more about prayer in the next study. Thinking through the following questions will help you prepare for the session. Did you ever have a friend or family member who seemed to be always asking you for things? What was missing from that relationship? What do you like most about your current prayer life? What do you like least?

PRAYER

Close with a prayer or ask someone in the group to do so.

Let's Pray

The purpose of this study is to help your group members develop a more balanced prayer life.

As people begin to take prayer seriously, the typical starting point is asking for things. While God invites us to approach him with our requests, there is much more to prayer than merely asking favors of God. This may become more apparent as you consider the parallels to a human relationship. For instance, what kind of friend only talks to you when he wants something? True friendship involves supporting, affirming, sharing, admitting wrongs, and expressing thanks. Similarly, our prayer life needs to broaden as we develop our friendship with God. A simple method called A.C.T.S. (adoration, confession, thanksgiving, and supplication) will be presented in this study. It will help your group members establish a pattern for more in-depth times of prayer.

PRAYER

Open the meeting with prayer.

OPENER

Use these statements to stimulate discussion:

Before becoming a Christian, my biggest misconception about God was _____.

The one aspect of God's character I have the most difficulty understanding is _____.

Note: Be careful not to attempt to resolve each person's difficulty at this point. That is not the purpose of asking this question.

REVIEW

Bible

Ask the group what Bible discoveries they made from further study of how God answers prayer (no, slow, grow, go)?

Prayer

Ask group members about the areas of life in which they prayed for wisdom.

Scripture Memory

Review Philippians 4:6-7

PURPOSE

When you took industrial arts or home economics in junior high or middle school, the assignment you did for the grade was also something you could take home and use. Perhaps you made a book rack or a blouse or even something good to eat. Learning about prayer is similar. In this study you will not only learn an effective way of praying, but you will also practice praying—and God will give you his answers "to take home with you"!

This study will show you a simple method for a more balanced prayer life. The first part will present the A.C.T.S. outline to help you structure your prayers. This will allow you to overcome the natural tendency to pray only about things you want. The second part will allow everyone to practice the A.C.T.S. pattern for prayer.

Begin with a short review of last week's session.

What are some principles of prayer you learned in the previous study? (Romans 8:26-29)

- The Holy Spirit helps us to pray

- The Holy Spirit intercedes for us

- Prayer comes from the heart

- Prayer is always answered: no, slow, grow, or go

A.C.T.S.: A Way to Pray

Adoration (Psalm 100:1-5)

In this step, we focus on the qualities and characteristics of the God to whom we're talking. It is very much like two people in love simply glorying in what they like about the other person and telling them so. It is slightly different from thanksgiving in that we focus on who God *is,* not just what he has *done* for us. Typically adoration and praise do not come easily for most of us.

How do you express adoration?

Through worship, song, thanks, and praise. If they struggle for answers, have them look at Psalm 100:2-4.

What benefits come to us from praising God?

They may mention encouragement, joy, spiritual growth, and so on.

Example of a Prayer of Adoration:
Lord, I praise you for being patient with me. How long you have waited for me to come to you! I ignored your voice, but you didn't give up. Your patience with me led to my salvation. This past week you demonstrated patience with me as I struggled with my own temper at home. Your patience is truly infinite. It is pure. It is active. It is perfect. I praise you and thank you for your patience with me!

Confession (1 John 1:9)

The hardest part about confession is the honesty it requires. Of course, we don't *inform* God of anything during confession—he knows everything already. We *agree* with God that what he saw and already knows about us, we now see and know.

Why is it difficult to confess our sin to God?

> Our natural tendency is to hide from God (and ourselves). In other words, we rationalize.

What does God promise he will do when we confess our sin?

> Forgive our sin.

> An optional question for more advanced groups could be: **How detailed should we get about confession?**

> Example of a Prayer of Confession:
> Heavenly Father, nothing is hidden from your sight. My sin doesn't surprise you, it just grieves you. My selfishness is your hurt. I have been caught up in longing for the material things I don't have rather than thanking you for what I do have. Because of what Christ did on the cross, I claim forgiveness. I will never have to bring up the specific instances of yesterday ever again—your forgiveness is complete.

Thanksgiving (Luke 17:11-19)

What excuses keep you from giving thanks to God?

> Example of a Prayer of Thanksgiving:
> Thank you, Lord, for revealing your presence in all you do. You have truly done many great things. You have saved me. You have given me a spiritual home—in heaven with you, on earth with your church. You have surrounded me with people who love me. Love and comfort are available anytime I need it. Thank you for these spiritual and relational blessings.

Supplication (Philippians 4:6-7)

What are some specific examples of requests we can bring to God in prayer?

> Asking probably comes easiest for most of us. That's why this step comes last. One of the wonders of the Christian life is that although God reigns as King over the universe, He delights to allow us to participate in the unfolding of His will. Through supplication, we let our needs—personal and even global—be made known to God.

If God knows all of our needs, why should we specify them through prayer?

> Among the reasons you might list:
>
> • he doesn't force his fellowship on us
>
> • we benefit from his fellowship
>
> • as he responds to our prayers, we grow in faith

- he receives credit for answers

- we benefit from participation in the process

What role does faith play in supplication?

Without faith (trust) there is no pleasing God. Faith is not the presumption that God will do the things we want. It's assurance that God will do what is best for us.

Example of a Prayer of Supplication:
Father I pray you would work in the lives of our national leaders. Guide them on a course of righteousness for our country. Lead them also to influence other nations for justice and peace. Protect the leadership of our church, spiritually, physically, in all ways. I also pray for Wendy's surgery. Give the doctors wisdom, and her courage. Help her family through this event. Help my sister Georgia cope with her new responsibilities at work as well as at home. Help us with our financial responsibilities, Lord. keep us from being greedy or careless. Make me a fruitful servant today.

For further study: 1 John 5:14-15

Prayer Time

Spend some time in prayer as a group to practice using the A.C.T.S. format.

Adoration

Go around the circle. Have everyone pray, completing the sentence,

Father, I want to praise you for being _____.

After everyone has prayed, you may want to play a song from a praise tape and encourage the group members to worship silently along with the tape. Then go on to:

Confession

What are some examples of sinful behavior, thoughts, or attitudes Christians should confess?

You should lead in a general prayer of confession for the group. Allow all to silently "agree with God" about their sins. Close this time with verbal assurance of forgiveness, based on God's promise of cleansing through Christ's blood.

Thanksgiving

Go around the circle. Have everyone pray, completing the sentence,

Thank you, Lord, for giving me _____.

Supplication

What one or two major concerns are on your mind today?

> As people answer, have someone pray a short prayer for them. Then ask the next person to share. You should close this time of supplication with a short prayer thanking him that we can go to him with all of our requests.

YOUR WALK WITH GOD

Bible

Study James 4 noting observations and applications.

Prayer

Practice each of the four aspects of prayer—one each day.

Day One: Praise God using Psalm 23.

Day Two: Identify the main areas of temptation you struggle with. Confess any sin in these areas and pray for strength.

Day Three: Recall several spiritual, physical, and relational blessings. Thank God for each one.

Day Four: Pray for any major concerns in your life and in the lives of others who are close to you.

Scripture Memory

Be joyful always; pray continually; give thanks in all circumstances, for this is God's will for you in Christ Jesus. 1 Thessalonians 5:16-18

In the next study we will examine how regular quiet times can enhance your walk with God. To prepare for the session, ask yourself the following questions: What is one area of your walk with God with which you could use some help? What would be the consequences if the Holy Spirit were not in your life at all?

PRAYER

Close with a prayer or ask someone in the group to do so.

Getting Together with God

The purpose of this study is to help your group members establish the discipline of personal devotions, also known as quiet time.

A simple definition of quiet time is unhurried time with God, consisting of Bible study and prayer. Despite the simplicity of this definition, group members may ask, "When I start having these quiet times with the Lord, how do I know I'm doing this right?"

The best personal devotions are those that allow an individual to develop his or her relationship with God. Quiet times are simply appointments with God—a way to spend a small amount of uninterrupted time together.

The trouble with some of the existing "formulas" for quiet time promoted by others is that they are not perfectly suited to all individuals. Our philosophy is that there is no one best way to have a quiet time. Your group members should use an approach that works for them and is appropriate for their life situation.

PRAYER

Open the meeting with prayer.

Use these statements to stimulate discussion:

A word or phrase that describes what has been happening with me since the last meeting is _____.

Since our group began, I have been unexpectedly pleased with _____.

Bible

Ask the group about the observations and applications they made from James 4:1-17.

Prayer

Ask group members about their experience with the A.C.T.S. format for their prayer.

Scripture Memory

Review 1 Thessalonians 5:16-18.

After driving through miles of gridlock to arrive early to work, a busy executive closes his office door to enjoy a few moments of quiet before the phones begin ringing. . . . A frazzled mother puts her noisy children to bed and plops down on the couch in the stillness of the evening to talk at last with her husband. . . . A weary student takes a break from a frantic exam schedule to take an unhurried walk around campus.

What do all these people have in common? They need times of quiet and calm to relax, think about the day, and to build relationships with friends and family. In a similar way, we also need times of quiet and prayerful reflection with the Lord and his Word to build our relationship with him.

How do we do that? Scheduling regular quiet times is a good way to start. This lesson will give you some practical advice for establishing regular times for personal devotions.

What Is a Quiet Time?

How would you describe a good quiet time?

Simply defined, a quiet time is an appointment with God during which we pray and read or study the Bible. God talks with us and we talk with him.

What do you do during your times alone with God?

Have them share their routine (if they have one). It's worthwhile to talk over different ideas of what we can do during our appointments with God so that the time is spent in a meaningful way.

For further study: Some advanced groups may want to take a look at Jeremiah 31:33-34 for connections between the New Covenant and the discipline of personal devotions. Whereas before the Israelites had a written law that described God's character and his expectations, in the New Covenant, his law would actually dwell within the hearts of his children. No more intermediaries would stand between people and God, because everyone would be in intimate communion with him. Spending time alone with God probably best exemplifies this new aspect of our walk with him and his closeness to each of us.

Making the Time

Why is it difficult for us to find time for personal devotions?

Too busy, too noisy, no scheduled reading plan, and so on.

Here are some ways to find time in a crowded schedule:

- Listen to a cassette tape of worshipful music as you drive, work around the house, or get ready for the day.

- Take a walk or ride in the car to a forest preserve, the country, or other place of natural beauty.

- Sing worshipful songs to the Lord.

- Occasionally vary your quiet time routine so that you don't get stuck in a rut.

What could you do to make your times alone with God more meaningful?

> Find a quiet place, select a time of the day when you are alert, use a devotional plan or other helps, and so on.

Studying the Bible

What hinders you from getting more out of personal Bible study?

> Don't understand the background of the book, don't know how it applies to today's circumstances, time constraints, and so on.

Here are some ways to vary your study of the Scripture:

- Use a concordance to study a specific topic, character trait, or Bible character.

- Use the cross references in the margin of your Bible to study a topic.

- Meditate on a passage by creating vivid mental pictures of the story or event.

- Rewrite the passage, using contemporary wording or your own circumstances as the setting.

- Mark interesting phrases that stand out to you.

- Write down questions as you read.

- Write a short title to describe the passage you are reading.

- Listen to the Bible on tape.

What are some other creative ways of making your Bible study more meaningful?

> Use an understandable version, read whole books at a time, study for a longer sitting peroidically, use a commentary or study Bible, and so on.

Praying

What prevents you from praying consistently?

Too busy, distracted by duties in life, lack of faith in the value of prayer, and so on.

Here are some other variations you can use to keep your prayer life fresh:

- Write out your prayers.

- Keep a prayer journal to record your prayers and answers.

- Vary the A.C.T.S. pattern so that you spend one day in adoration, another in confession, and so on.

- Put away your prayer list and simply talk to God.

- Vary your position, posture, or location when you pray.

What other ideas do you have to make your prayer time more effective?

Action Plan

What is the best time of day for you to have your quiet time?

What is the best place for you to have your quiet time?

> Examples could be at the kitchen table, in the car or on the train, at your desk at work, in your favorite chair at home.

What are the most likely distractions or interruptions you will face?

> Children needing attention, someone coming by to talk, falling asleep, telephone calls.

What can you do to prevent these distractions or interruptions?

> Preventative measures could include using an answering machine, finding a better location, asking for your spouse's cooperation, and so on. What they all have in common is planning.

BOTTOM LINE

**Getting together with God on a regular basis is
essential to your spiritual growth.**

Bible

Study James 5:1-20, noting observations and applications.

Prayer

Pray that you may become the kind of person who does what the Bible says (James 1:22).

Scripture Memory

Review the verses from the previous three studies: Psalm 119:11; Philippians 4:6-7; 1 Thessalonians 5:16-18.

Next time we will begin the first of four studies on the Holy Spirit. To prepare, recall how you first learned about the Holy Spirit.

PRAYER

You should close with a prayer, incorporating what members have shared about their future hopes for their times with God.

9

The Role of the Holy Spirit

The purpose of this study is to help your group members understand the person and work of the Holy Spirit.

"The Christian life is not difficult—it's impossible. The only one who could live it is Christ himself. So if we're to live the kind of life he did, we'll have to have him living his life through us." While this statement could be misunderstood to imply that the Christian life consists of total passivity, when properly applied this concept affirms a great truth. Without the ministry of the Holy Spirit, the Christian will be very frustrated in his or her attempts at growth and service. By understanding and appropriating the Spirit's work, great fruitfulness results. With this goal in mind we now embark on a four-week emphasis on the role of the Holy Spirit.

You or a group member should open the meeting with prayer.

Ask:

If you could go to anywhere in the nation for a free vacation, where would you choose? Explain.

My favorite way to waste time is _____.

Bible

Have group members talk about the observations and applications they made from James 5:1-20.

Prayer

Ask the group members about how the words of James 1:22 affected their prayers this week.

Scripture Memory

Review Romans 8:28; Philippians 4:6-7; and 1 Thessalonians 5:16-18.

PURPOSE

Think for a moment about the way wind affects our lives. It is often a gentle current that refreshes us on a hot day. It is the steady breeze that keeps a child's kite aloft and guides a sailboat to its destination. Then, too, the wind can be a tremendous force of nature, whipping snow into gigantic snow drifts, knocking down power lines, and grounding airplanes. We must learn to respect its power or we may find ourselves in danger.

Jesus compared the Holy Spirit to wind (see John 3:8). Like the wind, the Spirit can assist us in our efforts to please God, and he also intervenes to discourage us from sinful activity. His power must not be resisted, however, because to do so affronts God and cuts us off from our source. Cooperation with the Holy Spirit is essential for any Christian's walk with God. Who is the Holy Spirit and what does he do? This study will help you understand the person and work of the Holy Spirit.

Who Is the Holy Spirit?

Read John 14:16-26.

What titles does Jesus use to describe the Holy Spirit? (John 14:16-17)

> Counselor, Spirit of Truth,
>
> Note: Notice the passage says "he," not "it." The Holy Spirit is a person, not a force.

Who sent the Holy Spirit? (John 14:26)

> The Father, in Jesus' name

Why can't the world accept the Spirit? (John 14:17)

> The world neither sees him or knows him.

What Is the Role of the Holy Spirit?

In what way does the Holy Spirit convict us? (John 16:7-11)

- Convicts sinners of their unbelief (sin)
- Reminds us of God's purity (righteousness)
- Assures us of God's eventual triumph over evil (judgment)

How does the Holy Spirit guide us? (John 16:12-15)

> He guides us into truth, especially truth about Jesus

In what way does the Holy Spirit teach us? (John 14:26)

> He reminds us of God's Word (similar to what Jesus did after His resurrection in Luke 24:27, 32, 44-45).

How does the Holy Spirit help to save us? (Titus 3:5)

> He acts in our conversion (and then helps us grow).

What does it mean when we say the Holy Spirit reassures us? (Romans 8:15-16)

Affirms that we belong to God as his children.

Note: The Aramaic word "Abba" is translated literally as "Daddy." It is what a little child would call his father, especially in times of need (see Mark 14:36, Galatians 4:6).

In what way is the Spirit like a deposit? (Ephesians 1:13-14)

He seals us in the Father. He is the pledge (down payment) by God to us that the full inheritance awaiting us in heaven will be received someday. (Note John 10:27-30 about how secure we can feel in this promise.)

For what does the Holy Spirit empower us? (Acts 1:8)

He is the source of power in witnessing.

How does the Holy Spirit help us when we pray? (Romans 8:26)

He prays on our behalf.

For further study (if time is available):

Where does the Holy Spirit live? (1 Corinthians 6:19-20)

As Jesus had promised, the Holy Spirit is in us. God's presence is now literally within every believer.

What else does the Holy Spirit give us? (1 Corinthians 12:1-7)

He distributes spiritual gifts for service to the church.

What does the Holy Spirit produce in us? (Galatians 5:22-23)

He also produces in us His fruit—those qualities that make us like Jesus.

Note: "Fruit" is singular—these qualities are all aspects of one thing and are all equally necessary to our growth in Christ. The Holy Spirit will produce all the fruit, not just part.

What else does the Holy Spirit do for us? (Galatians 5:16-18)

He leads us (in this context, he leads us primarily toward holy character, but this principle would extend to other kinds of choices as well, e.g., major decisions, occupation, finances, relationships, and so on.

What role of the Spirit impressed you in this study?

How would you summarize the ministry of the Holy Spirit to a new Christian?

He is the third person of the Trinity. He is God. He lives in us to produce life changes so we become more like Christ.

Bible

Study Philippians 1:1-30 three times this week.

Prayer

Day One: List temptations you face and write down what you could do to better resist them.

Day Two: List some physical or material blessings (ones you normally don't think of).

Day Three: Pray about a major concern in your life.

Scripture Memory

Do not get drunk on wine, which leads to debauchery. Instead, be filled with the Spirit. Ephesians 5:18

In the next study we will discover what it means to be filled with the Holy Spirit. To prepare, ask yourself: What are some things that can fill or dominate a person's life? Also, if the Holy Spirit is in our lives as Christians, why don't our lives reflect Jesus Christ more clearly?

Close in prayer, emphasizing appreciation for the person and work of the Holy Spirit.

Being Filled with the Holy Spirit

10

OVERVIEW

The purpose of this study is to help your group members understand what it means to be filled with the Holy Spirit.

When a person talks of "filling" something, we often see in our minds the image of fluid being poured into a container. Unfortunately, many Christians imagine that "being filled with the Holy Spirit" is much the same process. They see themselves as vessels into which God pours a "measure" of the Holy Spirit. This image confuses people, for it does not accurately depict what it means to have the Holy Spirit fill us in a biblical sense. This study clarifies what being filled with the Holy Spirit entails and spells out what his work in us accomplishes.

PRAYER

You or a group member should open the meeting with prayer.

OPENER

Ask the following questions:

What is the most memorable gift you ever received as a child?

What is the most daring thing you have ever done? What made it so daring?

Bible

Review Philippians 1:1-30, having group members list their observations and applications.

Prayer

Temptations: Don't ask them for specifics, but ask if praying about temptations helped in any way.

Blessings: Ask group members to recall some of the blessings they thanked God for last week.

Concerns: Share one of your own with the group (also, have everybody write down each other's concerns during this time). Briefly pray for the concern expressed by the person on your right.

Scripture Memory

Review Ephesians 5:18.

PURPOSE

Note: Leaders, you may actually want to demonstrate the following illustration rather than just read it.

Imagine filling two glasses with equal amounts of water. Into one glass you drop a seltzer tablet that is wrapped in a plastic bag. You notice that nothing happens—the plastic has prevented the tablet from dissolving in the water. Now you drop an unwrapped tablet into the other glass. The tablet fizzes exuberantly and fills the glass with hundreds of small bubbles.

This simple experiment illustrates how we should allow the Holy Spirit to work in our lives. When we do not face our sin and hinder his work, our disobedience acts like the plastic bag around the seltzer and robs us of the Spirit's dynamic influence. But when we are receptive and obedient to God, the Holy Spirit releases his energy into every part of our life. This study will show you how the Holy Spirit can fill your life and what his work in you accomplishes.

To review the study from last week, ask your group members:

How did we describe the role of the Holy Spirit in the last study?

If group members are stuck for answers, have then turn back and look in their study guides.

What is the Holy Spirit's role in the process of our spiritual growth? (Philippians 1:6)

He will carry it on to completion.

What is our role in the process of spiritual growth? (Ephesians 5:18)

Be filled with the Holy Spirit and hasten this process.

What does it mean to say that Christians should be "filled" with the Holy Spirit?

"Filled" in this sense means basically the same thing as when we say, "He was filled with rage." Similar expressions include "controlled by," "under the influence of," "captivated by," and "dominated by."

Note: The comparison to being drunk found in Ephesians 5:18 is illustrative. When someone is drunk he or she is said to be "controlled by," under the influence of," "captivated by," or "dominated by" alcohol. A person who is drunk also walks differently, talks differently, thinks differently, treats people differently, loses his inhibitions, and in short seems like a different person. In a similar way, the person who is controlled by the Holy Spirit is still the same person but shows a markedly different behavior.

What are some things being filled with the Spirit helps us to do? (Ephesians 5:19-21)

Build up others; worship, express thankful hearts, show a submissive attitude toward others.

How does being filled with the Spirit influence our character? (Galatians 5:22-23)

As the Holy Spirit is allowed to "spread out" within our lives, we will change so that his qualities will become ours.

Note: Questions may arise about the baptism of the Holy Spirit. Some Christians teach that believers do not necessarily receive the Holy Spirit at conversion (as in Acts 2). It's important to remember, however, that you cannot be a Christian without having the Holy Spirit in you (Romans 8:9), so if you still need the Holy Spirit, you also still need Christ. The ability to receive and affirm Christ is a work of the Holy Spirit (John 3:5-7; 1

Corinthians 12:3); through him, Christ comes in us. By the Spirit's agency, we're placed into the body of Christ; so through him, we become in Christ. Recall that in the illustration about the seltzer tablet, the tablets were placed in both glasses. If you've truly received Christ, you already have the Holy Spirit. The Bible tells us to seek to be filled with (or controlled by) the Spirit who is already in us.

Recall the opening illustration. What does the plastic bag around the seltzer tablet represent?

Sin or reluctance to let God into certain areas of our lives.

What would cause you to seal in or limit the power of the Spirit in your life?

Selfishness, lack of faith, not trusting in God, and so on.

How do we "unwrap" and turn loose the Holy Spirit's influence in us?

Submit, cooperate with, yield to, follow the Holy Spirit; replace the old self with the new self; do things his way, not your way.

In what areas have you allowed the Holy Spirit to permeate your life?

Be prepared to share a personal example.

BOTTOM LINE

Let the Holy Spirit's influence permeate your entire life.

YOUR WALK WITH GOD

Bible

Study Philippians 2:1-30, making at least three applications and observations.

Prayer

Day One: Adoration—meditate on Psalm 103:1-5 and write out a prayer of adoration in your own words.

Day Two: Thanksgiving—thank God for relationships with specific people that have been a blessing to you and others.

Day Three: Concerns—pray for three of your own and three from other people (you may pray about the concerns shared at the beginning of this study).

Scripture Memory

I have been crucified with Christ and I no longer live, but Christ lives in me. The life I live in the body, I live by faith in the Son of God, who loved me and gave himself for me. Galatians 2:20

In the next study we will look at how believers can be filled with the Spirit. Consider these questions: Describe something that is now a habit for you that had to be learned over time. How did that behavior, practice, or discipline become second nature? As a Christian, what changes in your life have come easily? What changes have come with difficulty? What changes aren't coming at all?

PRAYER

Close the meeting with a prayer.

How to Be Filled with the Holy Spirit

This study will help your group members understand how they can live in the Spirit more fully each day.

Two things are important to get across in this study. First, conveying to your group exactly what it means to be filled with the Spirit must be a priority, since some members may not have a clear understanding of this idea. Second, group members need to retain the simple steps introduced by this study so that they can maintain a pattern of daily interaction with the Holy Spirit.

PRAYER

Open with prayer.

OPENER

Have the group complete one or both statements:

My favorite day this week was _____ because _____.

The thing I value most in a friendship is _____.

Bible

Go over their observations and applications from Philippians 2:1-30.

Prayer

Ask group members to read their paraphrases of Psalm 103:1-5. Also have them name the people they were thankful for or share any answers received to last week's concerns.

Scripture Memory

Have group members recite Galatians 2:20.

PURPOSE

A brash young entrepreneur decides to start a business in a lucrative, high-tech field. Because he needs the help, he brings on board a top-flight consultant to function as his daily advisor. But instead of trusting in the consultant's wisdom, the entrepreneur decides to do things his way. He ignores directives about financial planning. He makes ill-advised decisions without his advisor's knowledge. He even keeps him out of important meetings. Predictably, the business fails within a short time.

Many Christians fail to realize that their relationship with the Lord shares many of the same problems. These people know about the wisdom of a daily quiet time and may even want the Spirit to direct their lives. But they insist on doing things their own way. It comes as no surprise that they stumble again and again. These setbacks are entirely preventable, however. This study will show you how you can live in the Spirit more fully each day.

To review the study from last week, ask: What changes in your life will occur as a result of being filled with the Holy Spirit?

We can build up others; worship; express thankful hearts; show a submissive attitude toward others.

How Can I Be Filled with the Holy Spirit?

1 Surrender to Christ

What are Christians to put to death? (Colossians 3:1-5)

Sin, their earthly nature, and the desires of the flesh.

For further study: Romans 6:6-11; 7:4-6

What does it mean for a Christian to become a living sacrifice? (Romans 12:1-2)

To act and think in a manner holy and pleasing to God; to not conform to the pattern of this world, to renew our minds according to his will.

Read both Luke 18:22-23 and 19:5-8. How would you compare the ways in which these two men faced the need to surrender to God?

The rich young ruler was sad about his situation but refused to submit; Zacchaeus gladly conformed to God's demands.

Note: To clarify what it means to surrender, explain that we die to sin and die to "self-will"—the desire to control our lives without inference from God.

Self-Directed Living

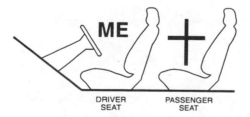

DRIVER SEAT   PASSENGER SEAT

Explanation of diagram: The circle stands for our lives—all of the characteristics of our existence. In this illustration the self is in the driver's seat, controlling the life with little or no direction from God. Christ is in the life—the person is a born-again Christian—but he is not "steering" the life of the believer.

What problems will result from a self-directed life?

Without Christ as the controlling and transforming force, we are doomed by our sinful nature to live a life that is self-centered and defeated.

Spirit-Directed Living

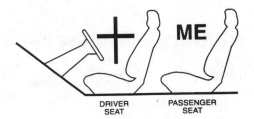

Explanation of diagram: Christ is now truly Lord of the person's life. The self, though present, has been moved to the passenger seat. The fruit now evident results from the transforming work of the Spirit. Some of the changes begin immediately, although the full maturing of these qualities requires a lifetime.

What traits will a Spirit-directed life produce?

It is only through our submission to the renewing power of the Spirit that we are able to become the kind of people who are pleasing to God.

2   Obey Christ

Once you have surrendered (an inward change) the next step is to obey (an outward change).

What happens when Christians surrender but do not obey? (1 John 2:3-6)

They remain insincere, incomplete people.

List a few areas of your life that are important to you. What does it mean to obey Christ in each area?

Members could talk about money, children, marriage, leisure, work, relationships, the future, possessions

3   Abide in Christ

To abide in Christ means to continue or remain in him. Why is abiding in Christ important? (John 15:1-11)

So that we bear fruit and do not lose our connection withGod.

Note: There is no such thing as being filled with the Holy Spirit once and for all. Union with Jesus Christ is a day-to-day, even moment-by-moment connection with the Lord. As a branch is connected to a vine, so are we connected to and dependent on the Lord. As a branch can bear fruit only by relying on nutrients from the vine, so we too have to rely on him for spiritual nutrition. In Ephesians 5:18, the original Greek of the passage makes this ongoing nature of the ministry of the Holy Spirit clearer. The tense used (present imperative) conveys the sense of "continue to be filled, go on being filled" with the Holy Spirit.

How can you tell when you are not abiding in Christ?

Unwillingness to obey his commands, indifference to spiritual matters, and so on.

Conclusion

How can you live in the Spirit more fully each day?

A practical suggestion for walking in the Spirit is to start each day with a prayer of surrender, a request for power to obey, and an affirmation of your abiding relationship with Christ.

BOTTOM LINE

We are filled with the Spirit by surrendering, obeying, and abiding.

YOUR WALK WITH GOD

Bible

Do a study of Philippians 3:1-21 at least three times, noting observations and applications.

Prayer

Look up the following passages that relate to obeying Christ. On each of four days, pray for the two areas listed that should be surrendered to Christ's control.

Day One: The future (Proverbs 3:5-6; James 4:13-17) and relationships (Matthew 5:21-26; Romans 12:9-21)

Day Two: Work (Colossians 3:22—4:1; Psalm 127:1-2) and leisure (Mark 6:31-32; Ephesians 5:15-16)

Day Three: Marriage (Matthew 19:4-6; 1 Peter 3:1-9) and children (Colossians 3:21; Psalm 127:3-5) or, if you are single, another significant relationship.

Day Four: Money (Psalm 112:5; 1 Corinthians 16:1-2) and possessions (Matthew 6:31-33; Luke 12:13-21)

Scripture Memory

Anyone, then, who knows the good he ought to do and doesn't do it, sins.   James 4:17

Next time we will discuss how we can grieve the Holy Spirit—ways in which we hinder his work. To prepare, think about the different ways a person can suppress or extinguish a fire. What parallels can you draw between those conditions and the ways a believer can put out the fire of the Holy Spirit?

PRAYER

You should offer an example of a simple prayer of surrender on behalf of the whole group, coupled with a pledge of obedience and gratitude for God's allowing us to abide in Christ.

Grieving the Holy Spirit

OVERVIEW

The purpose of this study is to help your group members understand what it means to grieve the Holy Spirit and to help them know how to get back in step with the Spirit when they do.

If you "live by the Spirit . . . you will not gratify the desires of the sinful nature" (Galatians 5:16). Although what Paul said here is true, the problem is we don't always live by the Spirit—many times we hinder his work or even quench him. After the previous studies, your group should have a better sense of what it means to be filled with the Holy Spirit. It is just as important, however, for them to know what will shut out his power in their lives and how they can get back on track when they grieve him.

PRAYER

You or a group member should open the meeting with prayer.

OPENER

Have group members complete these statements:

The best way for me to describe last week is _____.

I could raise the quality of my relationship with the Lord if I _____.

Bible

Go over their observations from Philippians 3:1-21.

Prayer

Ask the group about their experience in praying for specific areas that need to be surrendered to the Lord.

Scripture Memory

Have group members recite James 4:17.

PURPOSE

Imagine that you are sitting around a campfire on a cool autumn evening. The warmth of the flames makes you feel comfortable and content. You become lost in your thoughts when, without warning, a sudden shower pours down on your campsite. The leaping flames soon turn into flickers, then become smoldering ashes. Now you are wet and miserable, and the chill of the evening makes you long for the glow that you felt a few moments earlier.

In much the same way, we can quench the fire of the Holy Spirit with careless actions and sinful attitudes. Not only do we cause God anguish, but we become miserable ourselves. This study will help you understand what it means to grieve the Holy Spirit and how to get back in step with the Spirit when you do.

STUDY

Grieving the Holy Spirit

What are some ways to cause a friend or parent to grieve?

Disobey parents, ignore or take advantage of a friend, and so on.

What does it mean to grieve the Holy Spirit? (Ephesians 4:29-31)

To sin—whether through unwholesome talk, anger, bitterness, or other actions displeasing to God.

What does it mean to put out the Spirit's fire? (1 Thessalonians 5:19–22)

We should not ignore or put aside the instruction the Spirit gives us.

Ways We Grieve the Holy Spirit

1 Active disobedience (sins of commission)

What are some example of active disobedience? (Galatians 5:16-21)

Sexual immorality, impurity and debauchery; idolatry and witchcraft; hatred, discord, jealousy, fits of rage, selfish ambition, dissensions, factions and envy; drunkenness, orgies, and the like.

For further study: 1 John 2:15-17 and 1 Corinthians 6:9-10.

Why does active disobedience grieve the Spirit?

It shows that we are continuing to regard our own authority and wisdom as greater than God's, and it harms greatly our witness in front of nonbelievers.

2 Passive disobedience (sins of omission)

What is passive disobedience? (James 4:17)

Inactivity becomes sin when a leading or command from God is ignored. It is important not to overlook this kind of sin, for it produces consequences similar to those produced by active disobedience.

What are some examples of knowing the right thing to do but not doing it?

If some of your group members are confused or need scriptural references, use some of the following:

- Not employing your spiritual gift (Matthew 5:16)
- Not being compassionate towards a needy brother or sister (James 2:15-16)
- Not tithing (Malachi 3:8)
- Withholding kindness toward family or friends (1 Timothy 5:8; Matthew 15:3-6)
- Not seeking ways to be a servant to others (Mark 10:42-45)
- Casual attitude towards attending church and small group meetings (Hebrews 10:25)
- Laziness (Proverbs 6:6-10)

3   Being ashamed of Christ

What consequences will a believer suffer for being ashamed of Christ? (Mark 8:38)

Christ will be ashamed of that person when he returns in glory.

In what situations do you find it difficult to stand up for Christ?

Be prepared to share a personal example to help the group members to open up.

For further study: Romans 1:16, 2 Timothy 1:8,12; Matthew 10:32-33

4   Lack of faith in Christ

Read Mark 9:17-23. Who lacked faith in this story?

The disciples

How should we respond when we lack faith? (Mark 9:24)

We should ask God to help us overcome our unbelief.

Why does lack of faith grieve the Holy Spirit? (Hebrews 11:6)

We cannot please God if we do not believe in the promises he has given us.

For further study: Mark 6:1-6; Hebrews 3:16—4:2; Matthew 6:25-34)

In what way do you frequently grieve the Holy Spirit?

Be prepared to answer this question, too.

What should we do when we think we are grieving the Holy Spirit?

The path back to being filled with the Holy Spirit is actually quite simple. After you acknowledge your sin (1 John 1:19), go back through the steps from the previous study: surrender to Christ; obey Christ; abide in Christ.

BOTTOM LINE

Sin hinders the work of the Holy Spirit in our lives.

Bible

Study Philippians 4:1-23 three times, writing down your observations and applications.

Prayer

Day One: Adoration—read Psalm 103:15-22 and praise God for his love and righteousness.

Day Two: Confession—pray about anything mentioned in this study that you feel convicted about. Be specific.

Day Three: Supplication—pray for members of your family who have emotional, physical, or relational needs.

Scripture Memory

Review the memory verses from the previous three studies: Ephesians 5:18; Galatians 2:20; James 4:17.

Next time we will review the previous topics in this study. To prepare, look back through studies 1–12. Which topic was most memorable to you? In what ways have you seen progress in your Christian life?

PRAYER

Pray that each member will keep in step with the Spirit and that God would remove any obstacles in each member's life that might hinder the Holy Spirit's work.

Reviewing Friendship with God

OVERVIEW

The purpose of this study is to help your group members assess what they've learned and how they've grown.

This meeting is the final one in the study guide *Friendship With God*. It is a time to look back, to observe spiritual progress, and to anticipate the coming weeks of exploring the life and ministry of Jesus Christ, which your group will examine in the next two study guides.

By now a sense of group unity and relational depth should characterize your group. You have covered some potentially life changing material over the past few months and shared much of your lives with each other during that time. Let this review strengthen what you have nurtured thus far.

PRAYER

Open with prayer

OPENER

Have each person finish the sentence:

I would like to see a documentary or read a biography of _____ because _____.

Bible

Review Philippians 4:1-23, noting your group's observations and applications.

Prayer

Have group members share a particular need that they prayed for last week.

Scripture Memory

Review Ephesians 5:18; Galatians 2:20; and James 4:17

PURPOSE

This review culminates your study of *Friendship With God,* the first book in the *Walking With God Series*. Use this time to reflect on your small group experience so far. This is also a time to appreciate and be grateful for what God has accomplished in you. This study will help you assess what you've learned and how you've grown.

STUDY

As you ask these questions, encourage your group members to think for a moment and give honest answers. No one should be forced to elaborate on an answer if he or she is obviously uncomfortable about doing so.

Since we began, what have you found to be the most positive aspect of these studies?

Identify a fresh insight or an old truth that has come alive through this study.

What area of your personal spiritual growth needs improvement?

How has your understanding of the Bible changed since you began this study?

What is one change you've noticed in your prayer life as a result of this study?

How would you describe the importance of quiet time to someone who just became a Christian?

What is the significance of the Holy Spirit in the life of the believer?

Currently, what is the greatest obstacle to your walk with God?

Ten years from now, what you like your walk with God to be like?

I would like everyone to pray for _____.

> When they have answered all the questions, pass out 3 x 5 cards and have each person write his or her name on the card. Collect the cards, shuffle them, and give one to each group member (no one should have their own name). As each person gives an answer for the last question, the one holding the card with that person's name should write those needs down on the card and pray for that person at least three times during the next week.

BOTTOM LINE

God has given everything, even his life, to walk with you. Will you walk with him?

YOUR WALK WITH GOD

Bible

Study three times Matthew 4:1-25 (in preparation for the first study in *The Incomparable Jesus*).

Prayer

Day One: Adoration—pray in accordance with Psalm 91:1-2.

Day Two: Confession—what is something you've found difficult to do in recent days that you know you should do?

Day Three: Thanksgiving—thank God for the promises he has given us about the future.

Scripture Memory

Review the following verses: Revelation 3:20; 1 John 5:13; 2 Timothy 3:16-17; Psalm 119:11; Philippians 4:6-7; 1 Thessalonians 5:16-18; Ephesians 5:18; Galatians 2:20; James 4:17.

PRAYER

Read Ephesians 3:14-21. Then lead the group in a time of short praise and thanksgiving.

ON YOUR OWN

Arrange a time to sit down with each group member individually over the next few weeks. (If your group is a couples group, have men meet with men, women with women, or couples with couples.) Have them discuss their perspectives on their spiritual growth as measured by the four categories listed below.

Self-Evaluation

Your group leader will be meeting with you to discuss your current spiritual condition and your hopes for growing in your faith. Please take some time to reflect honestly on where you stand right now within these four basic categories of Christian growth. Rate yourself in each category.

+   **Doing well. I'm pleased with my progress so far.**

✓   **On the right track, but I see definite areas for improvement.**

—   **This is a struggle. I need some help.**

A Disciple Is One Who . . .

Walks with God

To what extent is my Bible study and prayer time adequate for helping me walk with God?

Rating:

Comments:

Lives the Word

To what extent is my mind filled with scriptural truths so that my actions and reactions show I am being transformed?

Rating:

Comments:

Contributes to the work

To what extent am I actively participating in the church with my time, talents, and treasures?

Rating:

Comments:

Impacts the world

To what extent am I impacting my world with a Christian witness and influence?

Rating:

Comments:

Other issues I would like to discuss with my small group leader:

The
Incomparable Jesus

Experiencing the Power of Christ

Introduction

What do you do well? Most of us have some skill or distinguishing trait for which we're recognized. One person can work with cars, another person is knowledgeable about history, someone else has a great sense of humor. Some people are known for what they make, some for how they serve, some for what they do, others for what they say. God made us all different, and that differentness is shown in the gifts we bring to the rest of the world as we fulfill the potential vested in each of us by our creative Creator. We're able to become proficient as we cultivate, practice, and focus on those skills or areas of interest. Whatever captivates our minds and hearts—whatever becomes second-nature to us—eventually forms how we're perceived by the world around us. We become someone special to others by having something special to offer—all of which flows from being attracted to and spending time absorbed in a special area of interest.

What do you do well that you can offer in service to God? Is there anything you're known for that relates to eternal concerns? What has captivated your mind and heart—what has become second nature—that you can present to your world in a unique and purposeful way in the name of Jesus? The shared goal of every Christian, no matter how we're wired individually, is to become like Jesus. We will each have a unique gift to offer that will make us different, but we will all be striving for the same qualities when we strive after Christian character. We don't all need to be experts at the same thing—in fact, God designed the church, as we'll see in later books in this series, so that nobody would be an island of competence. But everyone who names the name of Christ must do as Christ did, and that can only happen as we become "experts" at knowing Jesus. Details of theology may seem tedious or even boring, but none of us should yawn when we say, "Jesus is Lord" and try to understand what that means. Others may spend hours drawing prophecy charts, but every one of us must draw on the power and wisdom of the One whose future reign over all is certain. We all have different "minors," but every believer must major on Jesus.

This study guide covers the preparations God made to send his Son into the world, and continues with discussions of the means and meat of his message. It is really the first of a two-part study on the life of Jesus completed in the next book in the *Walking with God Series, "Follow Me!"* Through these pages you'll discover anew the Messiah of Scripture and perhaps even revise some of your views of him. You'll take important steps toward a more accurate—and stronger—connection with the incomparable Jesus.

They Said He's Coming— The Prophecies

The purpose of this study is to help your group members understand how God prepared for the coming of Jesus Christ through Old Testament prophecies.

More than 300 Old Testament passages speak directly or indirectly of the coming of the Christ. They show us that Jesus was not merely in the right place at the right time but that he fulfilled God's plan as predicted and foretold hundreds of years before he was ever born.

Studying these prophecies is an exciting journey that will lead to a fresh discovery of God's power and wonder. Jesus fulfilled the details of all God's plans that were so clearly predicted—enabling him to care about all the details of our unpredictable lives.

PRAYER

Begin the meeting with a short prayer. This is what you should do first each week after everybody has arrived. It marks the formal beginning of every meeting.

To help warm up the group, ask:

What is something you've recently learned about yourself?

If your group is continuing from the previous study guide *Friendship With God,* use this review. Otherwise, skip ahead to Purpose.

Bible

Have your group members share their observations and applications from Matthew 4.

Prayer

Have group members share what aspects of their future they thanked God for. (Some examples might include: A home in heaven; provision for our needs throughout our lifetime; the eventual total defeat of Satan; new bodies at the resurrection; total emotional and psychological healing.)

Scripture Memory

See if your group can recite together all of the memory verses from *Friendship With God:* Revelation 3:20; 1 John 5:13; 2 Timothy 3:16-17; Romans 8:28; Philippians 4:6-7; James 4:8; Ephesians 5:18; Galatians 2:20; James 4:17.

Have your group members open their books to the first study. Then read the introduction, or have one of the group members read it while the others follow along.

Many Christians don't appreciate or understand the vital connection between the Old Testament and the New Testament. For example, there are over 300 prophecies in the Old Testament that refer specifically to the life of Christ! All of these prophecies came about just as predicted. This is especially amazing when you consider that more than 20 different authors wrote them over a 1,000-year period.

The probability of one person fulfilling just eight of the Old Testament prophecies is one in 10 to the 17th power, or one in 100,000,000,000,000,000 (one hundred million billion). The likelihood of accidentally fulfilling just 48 prophecies is one in 100 to the 157th power. Jesus fulfilled all 300. (See Peter Stoner's book, *Science Speaks*, Moody Press, 1963.)

These prophecies tell us a lot about Jesus. Through the prophets, God revealed many facts about Jesus' birth, life, and death. These signposts not only point to the Savior; they serve as proof of the divine origin of Scripture and confirm the divine nature of Jesus. To begin our study we will look up several prophecies and their fulfillment in the life of Christ.

STUDY

The Fulfillment of Prophecy

Read these prophecies to see the correlation between them and their fulfillment. Write down how Jesus fulfilled each prophecy.

> Have one group member look up the Old Testament reference and read it aloud. Have another group member read the corresponding New Testament reference. Allow the group members to supply the answers.

For more information about prophecies of Christ and how they were fulfilled, see *Evidence That Demands a Verdict*, by Josh McDowell.

What was to be unique about Jesus' birth? (Isaiah 7:14 and Matthew 1:18-25)

> He would be a son, born of a virgin, and divine.

Where was Jesus to be born? (Micah 5:2 and Matthew 2:1-6)

> Bethlehem.

How would Jesus be honored? (Psalm 72:10-11; Isaiah 60:6; and Matthew 2:11)

> Royal visitors would bring gifts.

Where would Jesus live as a young child? (Hosea 11:1 and Matthew 2:14-15)

> Egypt.

How would people be prepared for Jesus' public ministry? (Isaiah 40:3 and Luke 3:3-6)

> A messenger in the wilderness would announce his arrival.

Where would Jesus minister? (Isaiah 9:1-2 and Matthew 4:12-16)

> In Galilee.

What amazing feats would Jesus perform? (Isaiah 35:5-6 and Matthew 11:4-5; 15:30-31)

> Miracles of healing.

How would Jesus teach? (Psalm 78:2 and Matthew 13:34-35)

> In parables.

How would Jesus be received by others? (Isaiah 53:3 and John 8:48)

> He would be rejected.

For what price would Jesus be betrayed? (Psalm 41:9; Zechariah 11:12-13, and Matthew 27:3-10)

> Thirty shekels of silver.

> Background note: The prophecy about Jesus' betrayal found in Zechariah bears some explanation. In this passage, Zechariah told an allegory that pointed out how the people of Israel rejected the leadership that God had given him. As their "shepherd," Zechariah had been spurned, even though Israel still regarded him as a prophet who brought them God's revelations. In this respect, he resembled Jesus: The Good Shepherd who speaks for God. As the Jews in the Old Testament passage had paid Zechariah 30 shekels for what they thought the Word of God was worth, so the Jews in the New Testament paid 30 shekels for what they felt Jesus, the eternal Word of God, was worth. Then that "handsome price" (Zechariah 11:13)—note the sarcasm—was given in both cases to a potter through the temple.

> Compare also Exodus 21:32, where 30 shekels is the price of a slave.

How would Jesus respond to his accusers? (Isaiah 53:7 and Matthew 27:12-14)

> Silence.

How would Jesus die? (Psalm 22:14-18 and Matthew 27:33-44; John 19:17-18, 23-24, 28)

> By crucifixion.

Note: This is especially amazing in light of the fact that crucifixion wasn't even practiced when Psalm 22 was written!

How would Jesus be protected from physical harm? (Psalm 34:20 and John 19:32-36)

> He would have no broken bones (even though crucified).

What would Jesus' death accomplish? (Isaiah 53:4-6 and 2 Corinthians 5:21)

> Save us from our sins.

How would Jesus be buried? (Isaiah 53:9 and Matthew 27:57-60)

> Like a criminal, but in a rich man's grave.

What would happen to Jesus' body? (Psalm 16:9-10 and Acts 2:29-32)

> It would not decay.

> Note: If you have additional time, have the group look up the following prophecies and fulfillments:

Fact	Prophecy	Fulfillment
Jesus as both God and Man	Isaiah 9:6	John 1:1,14
Jesus from Seed of Abraham	Genesis 12:3;17:6-8	Matthew 1:1; Galatians 3:8, 16
Jesus from tribe of Judah	Genesis 49:10	Matthew 1:2; Revelation 5:5
Jesus from line of David	2 Samuel 7:12, 16	Luke 2:4
Jesus identifies with sinners	Isaiah 53:12	Matthew 27:38
Anointing of the Spirit	Isaiah 11:2	Matthew 3:16-17
Herod slaughters children	Jeremiah 31:15	Matthew 2:16-18
Triumphal entry into Jerusalem	Zechariah 9:9	John 12:13-14
Jesus as stumbling block to the Jews	Psalm 118:22	Matthew 21:42
Ascended to the right hand of God	Psalm 110:1	Matthew 22:41-45

The Value of Prophecy

Which of the prophecies about Christ has made the most significant impression on you in this study? Explain why.

Why is fulfilled prophecy important to Christianity?

> It proves the inspiration of Scripture, proves the existence of God, and shows the uniqueness of Christ.

How does fulfilled prophecy give you more confidence in God?

> It gives us reasons to worship God, helps us have courage in speaking with non-Christians about our faith, and encourages us to trust God.

BOTTOM LINE

Fulfilled prophecy shows us that Jesus is indeed the Christ (Messiah).

At the end of every study is a section called "Bottom Line." Each week you should read this summary sentence and have your group members write it down in their study guide word for word.

YOUR WALK WITH GOD

Make sure your group members understand the assignment for next week.

Bible

Set three appointments with God this week. Pick the times during the day that work best for you. Study Matthew 5 three times, noting specific observations and applications.

Prayer

Day One: Adoration—Using Psalm 119, worship God for the trustworthiness of his Word. Then take the chorus to the song, "God Is So Good," and write as many new verses as you can. (For example: God is so fair, God is so kind, God is my friend, He loves us so, I hope in him, and so on.)

Day Two: Confession—Look up Matthew 26:41. Pray for help in an area of frequent temptation in your life.

Day Three: Supplication—Pray for three of your most pressing concerns.

Scripture Memory

As part of the curriculum, we've included memory verses with each study. If you desire to make this discipline part of your discipleship experience, begin by memorizing this verse:

Watch and pray so that you will not fall into temptation. The spirit is willing, but the body is weak. Matthew 26:41

In the next study we will explore the concept that Jesus was both fully God and fully human. To prepare, ask yourself the following questions. Why would Jesus' identity be such a controversial issue that people would kill him over it? If a Christian has the Holy Spirit living inside him, why isn't he considered divine like Jesus? What's the difference?

The assignment at the end of each study is designed to be done during the group members' quiet time. In fact, *their homework is a quiet time.* Whatever else this small group experience does for your group members, it will help them establish a habit of regular appointments with God.

To assist group members in organizing their homework, we've prepared the spiritual journey notebook called the *Walking With God Journal.* This journal includes instructions for how to have a quiet time and blank pages to write out their Bible study notes and prayers. Your group members may find this study tool useful as they meet with God each week.

PRAYER

Close with a prayer of thanks to God for the confidence we have through fulfilled prophecy.

If your group is just starting out and you sense the members would be uncomfortable praying out loud at this time, simply say a closing prayer yourself.

Make sure everybody knows the time and place for the next meeting. Remind them of the need for punctuality. (Did you end the meeting on time?) Serve refreshments (if it's not too late).

Jesus—
The God-man

OVERVIEW

The purpose of this study is to help group members understand that Jesus is both fully God and fully man, and discover how this affects our relating to him.

The idea that Jesus is both fully God and fully man may be new to some in your group. They may currently think that he is part God and part man, or possibly one of three modes that God assumes. Be sensitive to these and other misconceptions people have. The doctrine of the Trinity is difficult for most people to grasp, though the truth "Jesus is Lord" is at the very center of historic Christianity.

PRAYER

Open the meeting with prayer. Prearrange for someone else to pray or ask a group member who has willingly prayed before.

Bible

Have each person share one observation and application from Matthew 5. Optional: You can do this in a unique way by having everyone do a two-minute stick drawing that represents what he or she learned or applied.

Prayer

Have each person share one of his or her verses to "God Is So Good," and then sing the song as a group using all the verses.

Scripture Memory

Have each person recite Matthew 26:41.

PURPOSE

Think for a moment about a current political figure. What is your opinion of that person? Do other people agree with you? Chances are that every person you meet will have a different perspective. Some will think that he or she is fair-minded, upright, and responsive to the people; others will regard that person as inept, a captive of special interests, or even dangerous!

In much the same way, just about every person has an opinion of Jesus. Many believe he was a great teacher. Some believe he was a humble philosopher whose followers altered then propagated his ideas. Some believe he was our Savior. Some believe he rose from the dead; many do not. A variety of mistaken ideas about who Jesus Christ actually was still float around. As Christians, we have a special responsibility to get a clear and accurate view of Christ. Jesus is at the center of our faith; he—not our moral code, church, or beliefs—is what people reject when they reject Christianity. We are not just "God-ians," but "Christians." What's more, our understanding of Jesus determines how we interact with him, how we respond to him, and—in the end—whether we spend eternity with him. The first step in being true Christians, then, is to understand who Jesus is.

It's important to understand that Jesus is both fully divine and fully human. Throughout church history, heretics have denied one or the other aspect of his nature. This study will help you understand his dual nature and the implications for us.

STUDY

Jesus' Eternal Existence

What similarities and differences do you observe in Genesis 1:1-3 and John 1:1-3?

> Both passages tell of a creator, but in John we are told that the Word—Jesus—is the source of that creation.

What is Jesus' relationship to the creation? (Colossians 1:15-19)

> He existed before it, created it, and sustains it.

What did Jesus himself claim about his existence? (John 8:58)

> Before Abraham was born, he had always been ("I AM" parallels Exodus 3:14 and Isaiah 41:4, statements made by God himself).

When did Jesus share the Father's glory? (John 17:5) Why is this significant?

> Before the world began, Jesus and the Father coexisted.

What is the significance of the phrase Jesus used to describe himself in Revelation 1:8, 17 and 22:12-13?

> Alpha and omega are the first and last letters of the Greek alphabet. "I am the Alpha and Omega" is the equivalent of our expression "everything from A to Z." In other words, Jesus is declaring his eternalness.

Jesus' Divinity

Even more important than preexistence, the Bible also identifies Jesus as part of the one and only God. He is the second person of the Trinity.

What do you understand the Trinity to mean?

> Try not to be judgmental if their expressions are inadequate.

What mistaken ideas do some people have about the Trinity?

157

If your group is relatively unfamiliar with common misconceptions about the Trinity, summarize these ideas:

- The Trinity is *not* three separate Gods (Tritheism). This idea views Jesus as one of three Gods. The Bible teaches clearly that there is only one God.

- The Trinity is *not* simply one person who appears in three separate forms (Modalism). This idea views Jesus as one form or mode of God, rather than a distinct person. In reality, Jesus is one of three distinct persons who all exist at the same time.

- The Trinity is *not* a hierarchy of three unequal persons (Arianism). This idea views Jesus as partially God but not equal with the Father; a great and powerful god, but not the all-powerful God. The Bible teaches that Jesus and the Father equally share the divine nature.

What object lesson or illustration have you heard that helps you understand the concept of "Trinity"?

Again, depending on your group, the following illustrations may help:

- The Trinity is like water, which can exist as liquid, ice, or steam. The three are actually one substance and can exist together.

- The Trinity is like the sun; it exists as fire, light, and heat—inseparable, yet distinguishable.

- The Trinity can also be represented by a circle with three dots on it—one circle, three dots that share the circle (one God, three personalities that share the divine nature).

How is Jesus related to God the Father? (John 10:30)

He is one with the Father.

What divine qualities does Jesus have? (Hebrews 1:2-3)

- Son of God, heir of all things.
- Co-creator of the world.
- Radiance of God's glory.
- Exact representation of God's nature.
- Holds all of creation together.
- Co-rules with the Father.

What is Jesus' relationship to the angels? (Hebrews 1:4-6)

- He is as much better than the angels as the Father is.

> He has a more excellent name.

> Unlike any angel, God calls him Son.

> Angels worship him as well as the Father.

What other qualities does Jesus have that belong only to God? (Hebrews 1:8-12)

> An eternal throne.

> Pure love of righteousness and hatred of sin.

> Creator of heavens and earth.

Note: This verse as written in Psalm 102:24-27 is ascribed to the God of Abraham, Isaac, and Jacob, but the writer of Hebrews takes it to apply equally to Jesus.

Jesus' Humanity

In order to come to earth, what was Jesus required to do? (Philippians 2:7-8)

> Became a man.

> Humbled himself.

How do we know that Jesus experienced fatigue? (John 4:6)

We read that he sat down at the well because he was tired from the journey.

How do we know that Jesus experienced thirst? (John 4:7)

He asked the Samaritan woman to give him a drink.

How do we know that Jesus experienced anger? (John 2:14-17)

He drove the money changers out the market.

How do we know that Jesus had limited knowledge while on earth? (Matthew 24:36)

Jesus said that he did not know the day or hour of his return—only the Father knew.

How do we know that Jesus experienced temptation? (Luke 4:2)

We read in this verse that the devil tempted him for forty days and nights.

How do we know that Jesus experienced sadness? (John 11:35)

He wept because his friend Lazarus had died.

How do we know that Jesus possessed a fully human body? (John 1:14)

John tells us that the Word (God) became flesh and lived among us.

The Importance of Jesus' Identity

How does it help us to know that Jesus is fully God? (Hebrews 4:13-14)

- Strengthens our faith, since we know he is all-powerful.

- Increases our sense of accountability because we know we must give an answer to him for our conduct.

How does it help us to know that Jesus was fully human? (Hebrews 4:15-16)

- Helps us pray, since we know he can sympathize with our weaknesses.

- Helps us appreciate God's love.

What bearing does our belief about Jesus have on our salvation? (John 8:24)

> We will die in our sins if we don't believe what Jesus claimed about himself. (See also 2 Corinthians 11:3-4.)

BOTTOM LINE

Because Jesus is both fully God and fully man,
he understands us and helps us understand God.

YOUR WALK WITH GOD

Bible

Study Matthew 6 three times during your appointments with God this week and make three observations and specific applications.

Prayer

Day One: Adoration and Thanksgiving—Identify one truth in Matthew 6 for which you can praise and thank God.

Day Two: Confession—Read Hebrews 12:1-4; what do you learn from these verses about your struggle with sin? Review Matthew 26:41 (the memory verse from last week).

Day Three: Supplication—Call one person from the group—make it a surprise—and find out what were his or her three major requests from last week so you can pray for him or her.

Scripture Memory

Your attitude should be the same as that of Christ Jesus: Who, being in very nature God, did not consider equality with God something to be grasped, but made himself nothing, taking the very nature of a servant, being made in human likeness. Philippians 2:5-7

In the next study, we will take a look at the careful preparations that God made for the coming of Christ. To prepare yourself for the discussion, consider the reasons why God would want to be intimately involved even in matters relating to Jesus' birth and family of origin.

PRAYER

Close the meeting in prayer, or have a group member do so.

Countdown to His Coming

OVERVIEW

The purpose of this study is to help your group members understand that God personally prepared the world for Christ's coming.

Many people are familiar with the Christmas story, but few are as familiar with the way God prepared for it. This will probably be true of your group as well. Come to this meeting prepared to highlight how God went out of his way to inform and involve individuals in preparing for the coming of his Son.

PRAYER

Open the meeting with prayer.

REVIEW

Bible

Discuss the group's work on Matthew 6. Ask:

What observations and applications did you make?

What did you learn from reading Hebrews 12:1-4?

Prayer

Briefly discuss your group's prayer assignment. Ask these questions:

How did you react to the phone calls you made to each other?

What was difficult about it for you?

How was the exercise good or helpful?

Scripture Memory

See who can recite Philippians 2:5-7.

PURPOSE

When you were in school, you probably preferred the teachers who showed personal interest in you, ones who called you by your first name and talked with you on a personal level. The ones who simply lectured from the front and didn't connect with you in any way are likely a dim memory for you. We simply don't respond well to a teacher who refuses to enter our personal worlds, no matter how important the lesson he or she may convey to us.

In keeping his promise to send the Messiah, God went far beyond teaching a message; he became personally involved in the lives of individual people. He used a real, live pair of newlyweds named Mary and Joseph to be the parents of his Son, even to the point of sending angels to tell them what would happen and to warn them of dangers. Through these personal visits, he protected and guided them. God did not merely fulfill prophecy himself; he allowed others to participate in the sovereign plan he was unfolding.

This study will show how God prepared the way for Jesus to be born into the world. In this study, you'll see how God's involvement then demonstrates his ongoing desire to be personally involved in our lives today.

The First Promise: John the Baptist

Read Luke 1:5-25 together. Then discuss these questions:

Describe Zechariah and Elizabeth. (Luke 1:5-7)

- Zechariah was a priest.

- Both of them were of outstanding moral character.

- They had no children.

Note: Don't miss the parallel here to Abraham and Sarah and their future child of promise.

In your own words describe what happens to Zechariah in Luke 1:8-13.

Zechariah was attending to his duties in the temple when an angel appeared before him. He was taken by surprise and was obviously fearful (as most of us would be). But the angel announced that God had heard his prayers and would give him a son named John.

What do we learn about John the Baptist from this account? (Luke 1:13-17)

- He would be great.

- He would have exceptional spiritual character.

- He would prepare the way for Christ.

- He would be like Elijah.

How did Zechariah and Elizabeth respond to this good news? (Luke 1:18-25)

Zechariah was uncertain at first. Elizabeth gave glory to God.

What can we learn about our own responses to God from this story?

- God uses ordinary people—don't be surprised if he wants to use you.

- Sometimes its hard to believe God would really use us—don't let doubt stand in the way of his will.

- Be sure to give glory to God when his work is evident.

The Second Promise: Christ Himself

Have some members of the group turn to Luke 1:26-38 and others to Matthew 1:18-25. After reading the passages discuss the following questions.

What was the angel's message to Mary? (Luke 1:26-38)

- God was with her, and she had found special favor with him.

- Though a virgin, she would conceive a child miraculously.

- Her son would be the Son of God.

How did Joseph respond to the situation he found himself in? (Matthew 1:18-25)

- At first, he wanted out!

- He took Mary as his wife in spite of his doubts.

What are some of the similarities in the circumstances of John the Baptist's and Jesus' births? What are the significant differences?

Similarities:

- God sent the angel Gabriel to each of the people who would be entrusted with these special children.

- God chose people of strong character and faithfulness.

- God brought about his promises in extraordinary ways.

- The parents were told that Jesus and John the Baptist were destined for great things.

Differences:

- Zechariah did not believe and was struck dumb until John's birth; Mary accepted the angel's words: "May it be as you have said."

- The roles that Jesus and John would fulfill would be different.

Do Mary and Joseph's experience provide any lessons for us today?

Among the possibilities: We must trust God, even when the circumstances may seem impossible and intimidating to us. For as the angel declared, "Nothing is impossible with God."

The Promises Fulfilled

Have a volunteer read Luke 1:39-56.

What was the focus of Mary and Elizabeth's conversation? (Luke 1:39-45)

The special children God had revealed they would have and his grace in choosing them.

As you read Mary's song of praise, what does she say about God that is just as true today as it was then? (Luke 1:46-56)

> Any of the phrases from this beautiful psalm could be easily applied to our day. Make a list with your group members.

What did Mary say about God that especially applies to a need in your life? Describe how that statement could help you.

> You may want to point out the passages describing God's mercy, might, provision for needs, and faithfulness.

BOTTOM LINE

The same God who prepared others for the Messiah wants to be involved in your life in a powerful way.

YOUR WALK WITH GOD

Bible

Study Matthew 7 three times, noting observations and applications. Also study the "On Your Own" assignment for background on the four Gospels.

Prayer

Day One: Adoration—Pray using Psalm 113 as a guide.

Day Two: Confession—Review Matthew 26:41, the verse you memorized in the first study of *The Incomparable Jesus.* Jot down a brief log of the last 24 hours: What thoughts, words, or deeds did not please God?

Day Three: Thanksgiving—Make a list of all the circumstances you have going for you. Thank God for each item on your list.

Scripture Memory

In the past God spoke to our forefathers through the prophets at many times and in various ways, but in these last days he has spoken to us by his Son, whom he appointed heir of all things, and through whom he made the universe.   Hebrews 1:1-2

In the next study we will take a close look at the birth and childhood of Jesus. To prepare, think about the events surrounding the Christmas story. What was remarkable to you about Jesus' birth ?

ON YOUR OWN

Background on the Gospels

The first four books in the New Testament tell about the life of Christ. These are complimentary accounts—similar to four newspapers covering the same story, or four books about the same famous person. Each stands alone as an account of the life of Christ, and although they contain many of the same stories and teachings, they were directed to different audiences and written by different authors. Here are some of the similarities and differences between them.

Matthew

The Author:

- Was one of the original twelve disciples.

- Also called Levi.

- Mentioned in four lists of the Twelve:
  Matthew 10:3
  Mark 3:18
  Luke 6:15
  Acts 1:13

- Called to follow Jesus.
  Matthew 9:9-13
  Mark 2:14-17
  Luke 5:27-32

- He was a tax collector for the Romans.

- He wrote his Gospel around A.D. 70.

The Book:

Matthew wrote specifically to Jews and emphasized Jesus as king. His purpose was to show the Jews that Jesus fulfilled Old Testament prophecy. He presented Jesus' teaching topically and contrasted Jesus with the Pharisees—Jewish religious experts of the day.

Mark

The Author:

- Was a close companion of Peter; told his story through the eyes of Peter.

- Full name was John Mark.

- Was the son of a Mary whose house was a meeting place for the disciples (see Acts 12:12).

- Possibly was converted as a result of Peter's ministry.

- Is mentioned in 2 Timothy 4:11.

- Was a cousin of Barnabas.

- Wrote his Gospel around A.D. 60.

The Book:

Mark wrote mainly to the Romans and emphasized Jesus as servant. Mark recorded Jesus' actions more than his teaching and concentrated on his power and authority.

Luke

The Author:

- Mentioned only three times in the New Testament: Colossians 4:14 (called "the beloved physician"), Philemon 24 (Paul's "fellow worker"), and 2 Timothy 4:11 (with Paul right before his death).

- Was a Gentile (non-Jew).

- Was a companion of Paul's on his second and third missionary journeys.

- Wrote his Gospel around A.D. 80.
- Was in Caesarea from A.D. 58 to 60 while Paul was in prison. Since Jerusalem was only a few miles from Caesarea, this would have given him the opportunity to collect firsthand data about Jesus.

The Book:

Luke addressed his Gospel to "Theophilus." It was written to the Greeks, or Gentiles (non-Jews), emphasizing Jesus' humanity. His Gospel is scholarly and historical, dealing with human needs (such as the weak, the suffering, and the outcast) and presents the human side of the Son of God.

John

The Author:

- Isn't identified until the end of the book, where he calls himself the "disciple whom Jesus loved" (21:20, 24).
- Father's name was Zebedee (Matthew 4:21).
- Mother seems to have been Salome (Matthew 27:56; Mark 15:40). She may have been the sister of the Mary who was the mother of Jesus. If so, John was Jesus' cousin and could have known him since childhood.
- Was a fisherman.
- Was one of the three inner circle disciples.
- Wrote his Gospel, three epistles, and Revelation.
- Wrote his Gospel around A.D. 90.

The Book:

The Gospel of John is directed at a general audience and emphasizes the deity of Christ. It consists mainly of Jesus' discussions and conversations. John's purpose in writing is spelled out in 20:31: *"These are written that you may believe that Jesus is the Christ, the Son of God, and that by believing you may have life in his name."*

The Early Years

OVERVIEW

The purpose of this study is to help group members understand the importance of the birth and childhood of Jesus.

Be sensitive to group members who have never before grasped the importance of the circumstances surrounding Jesus' birth. In this study they should come to realize God's plan of salvation was unfolding even as Mary delivered her child in that Bethlehem stable.

PRAYER

Have a volunteer open the meeting with prayer.

REVIEW

Bible

Have each group member share one observation and application from Matthew 7.

Prayer

Ask the group what they thanked God for this past week.

Scripture Memory

Have each person recite Hebrews 1:1-2.

PURPOSE

Many people regard the Christmas story as a marvelous, heartwarming event—but one that has little relevance for understanding the life and mission of Jesus while he was on earth. To them, it is mere background or historical detail. What a shame! Because they haven't grasped the tremendous work that God accomplished at Jesus' birth and in his childhood, they often find it difficult to apply this portion of the Gospels to their lives.

But the events surrounding the life of Christ tell us what *happens,* not only what *happened.* The challenge for you is to ask what these events reveal about the character of God. By telling you about what God *did,* they will show you what God does *now.* Though his specific actions may vary throughout history, his character will always be consistent—faithful, powerful, sovereign, caring.

In this study, we will see God's faithfulness in the events that surround the birth and childhood of Jesus.

STUDY

The Birth of John the Baptist

What was the controversy surrounding John's name? (Luke 1:57-66)

> It was customary to name the son after someone in the family. Everyone expected his name to be Zechariah, but both parents would break family tradition in order to obey God.

What does Zechariah and Elizabeth's insistence on naming their baby John tell us about their character? (Luke 1:13)

> They were determined to obey the specific instructions God gave them. In the face of tradition and family pressure, it would have been easy to back down and go with the flow. Instead they recalled God's promises and honored his command.

Note: John's name meant "God has been gracious"—a good name for someone who would announce the coming our Savior. We can imagine too that every time Elizabeth and Zechariah used his name, they were reminded of God's special work in their lives.

What were the results of Zechariah's obedience? (Luke 1:63-67)

- His speech was restored.

- He praised God.

- He recognized God's plan for John.

- He was filled with the Holy Spirit.

- Others feared God.

What can we learn from this passage that applies to our lives today?

Obedience to God's Word should be the chief priority in the life of every Christian—even if it means encountering resistance. God will also do great things for us when we obey him; Zechariah discovered this truth personally. We should also keep in mind that our obedience can cause others to honor and worship God, as was the case with the neighbors who heard Zechariah prophesy.

The Birth of Jesus

As a group, read Matthew 1:18-25. Then discuss the following questions:

What additional light did Paul shed on Jesus' birth? (Romans 5:6; Galatians 4:4)

It happened at just the right time in history.

What do we learn from this passage about the kind of man Joseph was? (Matthew 1:19)

He was a man concerned about propriety and honor, about doing the right thing. Yet he was compassionate and wanted to spare Mary from public shame.

Note: Among the Jews, betrothal was far more formal and binding than the modern American custom of engagement. Betrothal was considered a part of the transaction of marriage, and was just as binding.

What does this passage teach us about the environment that Jesus would be raised in?

God chose a family for Jesus where he would see positive role models of virtue.

How might your response to the angel's announcement of Jesus' birth have been similar to the shepherds' reaction? (Luke 2:8-20)

Point out that the shepherds were frightened but did not hesitate to follow the angels instructions. They praised God after finding Jesus.

What was the significance of Mary's reaction to the events surrounding Jesus' birth? (Luke 2:17-19)

The passage says that Mary "treasured up all these things and pondered them in her heart." Certainly the shepherds' words must have been a comfort and a reassurance to her. She was a young woman, probably 16 or 17 years old, and the difficult journey to Bethlehem while pregnant must have been a great strain for her. What an affirmation it must have been for her to have these shepherds come from nowhere to assure her that God was still at work and that this child was indeed the Messiah!

Jesus' Infancy

Why is it significant that Luke includes an account of the child's circumcision? (Luke 2:21)

Luke is showing that Mary and Joseph were fulfilling a very significant ceremony in the eyes of God. Circumcision was an outward mark to be present on all the male members of God's covenant people (see Genesis 17:9-11). It showed God's *ownership*—the Jewish people's privileged position as his elected nation. It was a physical act that symbolized a spiritual truth, much like the sacraments of baptism and communion in the New Testament.

Why do you think God drew the magi to visit Jesus? (Matthew 2:1-12)

God wanted to include non-Jews in his kingdom—seekers from any background were welcome.

How did Jesus spend his early childhood? (Matthew 2:13-23)

Hiding from Herod in Egypt, and then in Nazareth.

Note: This fulfilled a prophecy that the Messiah would be called out of Egypt (Hosea 11:1).

Jesus' Childhood

What kind of religious training did Jesus probably receive? (Deuteronomy 6:4-7)

Instruction in the Law of Moses from his parents. Joseph and Mary's character undoubtedly influenced him as he grew up.

What do we know about Jesus' later childhood? (Luke 2:39-52)

He was once separated from his parents while talking with adults in the temple. They were impressed with Jesus' wisdom.

What do we learn about God and his Son from these details of the early years of Jesus' life?

- God can be trusted—he fulfilled the prophecies concerning Jesus.

- God is personal—in addition to sending his Son, he visited Mary, Joseph, Elizabeth, Zechariah, and the shepherds through angels, and led the magi to Jesus.

- Jesus is extraordinary—the fulfillment of God's plan to save us.

BOTTOM LINE

The birth and childhood of Jesus demonstrate God's sovereignty and faithfulness.

YOUR WALK WITH GOD

Bible

Study Matthew 8 three times, noting observations and making applications. Also read the material in On Your Own.

Prayer

Day One: Adoration—Identify five specific aspects of creation that point to God's creativity and thank him for them. In order to observe them firsthand, go for a walk and pray as you go.

Day Two: Confession—What progress are you seeing in the area of temptation with which you struggle? To what do you attribute this growth? If there is no progress, why not?

Day Three: Supplication—Write out a prayer about three major concerns in your life. When you are finished, be still for a few moments in God's presence, listening to him. Write down what he is impressing on you.

Scripture Memory

Review Matthew 26:41, Philippians 2:5-7, and Hebrews 1:1-2.

The next study will focus on Satan's temptation of Christ in the wilderness. To prepare, think about the greatest areas of temptation that you face at this time. What do you do to help you resist temptation?

ON YOUR OWN

Who was John the Baptist?

One of the most colorful characters in the New Testament is John the Baptist. John lived in the wilderness under rugged conditions. His appearance was striking, even strange. We read that his clothes were made of camel's hair and that he ate locusts and wild honey. But John made God's righteousness a public issue. His message could be summed up by the theme "repent and live righteously." He challenged those secure in their religious attitudes to abandon their sin or face judgment. By doing so he prepared the way for the One who would embody righteousness and deliver those who turned to God from that coming judgment.

John the Baptist was certainly an unusual person, but his life and message had a very positive effect on the people of his day—he took a stand, he was a man of convictions, he promised new life through repentance, he lived continuously filled with God's Spirit. These and other qualities made him highly esteemed by the masses. Just as John the Baptist paved the way for the Messiah on earth back then, the account of his life and actions can make a highway to prepare you for the work of Jesus in your life today.

There is a fine line between the truth that attracts and differences that repel! For many Christians, being different means being odd. Some will "major on minors"—in other words, they mark themselves by what they don't do: no smoking, no drinking, no card playing, and so on. Such behavior, however, isn't necessarily an indication of true spirituality. It is far better to develop an internal character that stands out. The watching world may then come to say "Christians are people who are compassionate and generous, who serve others and who are role models for upright living." They will say "Christians *are*" rather than "Christians *don't*."

What about you? Do people perceive you as different? In an attractive way? Remember that the kind of difference that brings people to God is found in the lives of servants like John the Baptist.

Who Were the Wise Men?

The wise men were students of the stars, or astrologers, who probably came from Persia (modern-day Iran). Because the Jews were one time under Persian rule, the Persians were probably familiar with the religion of the Jews and their Messianic hopes.

In seeking out the new born king, their first stop was not Bethlehem, but Jerusalem. They checked in with Herod, naively assuming he and his court would be excited about the Messiah. They were excited—but not in the way the wise men assumed. Insecure and treacherous, Herod planned to kill the child and eliminate a future rival. He asked the wise men to report back to him when they had found the Christ child so that he could "worship" too. But these men were warned in a dream not to go back to Herod and returned to their country via a different route.

Even though they were not Jews, the wise men were quick to realize the majesty and significance of Jesus' birth. They presented him valuable treasures and worshipped him. Their arrival was a foreshadowing of the good news that would soon be available to all people, regardless or race or culture, who trusted in Christ for salvation.

Who Was Herod?

Herod was given the title of king of the Jews by the Romans, but his title was never accepted by the people. He was consumed by worries over his own position and power. He had ten wives over the years, two of whom he had killed. He killed three of his own sons, plus his brother-in-law and one of his wife's grandfathers. The news about the baby born to be king threatened his already shaky security. Knowing this about his nature and character helps us to understand why he ordered that all baby boys under the age of two be killed.

The Temptation of Jesus

OVERVIEW

The purpose of this study is to help group members learn to deal with temptation in their lives from the way Jesus responded to temptation.

Be tactful and encouraging as you open this subject with your group. Some may take the subject of temptation too lightly and consider it a waste of time to take a close look at their own behaviors. Others may be struggling with chronic temptations; they need to see that there is a way out.

PRAYER

Open the meeting with prayer.

REVIEW

Bible

Note observations and applications from Matthew 8.

Prayer

Adoration: Ask your group what aspects of creation they thought of as pointing to God's creativity.

Confession: Invite volunteers to tell about areas of their lives in which they've seen progress against a particular temptation.

Supplication: Ask the following question:
What did God impress on you about the concerns you brought to him?

Scripture Memory

Invite your group members to recite one of the passages they have memorized so far—Matthew 26:41, Philippians 2:5-7, or Hebrews 1:1-2.

PURPOSE

We all struggle with temptation. The specific temptations each of us faces differs from person to person, but none of us escapes all of them. And whether or not we ask God to save us from it, it always returns. We seem never to be done with our evil desires.

What can we do about temptation? Centuries ago Martin Luther said, "You cannot keep birds from flying over your head, but you can keep them from building a nest in your hair!" Temptations, like birds in the air, will always be with us. But we should not, nor do we have to, allow them to "roost." We can resist.

Jesus faced temptation countless times. We can learn a great deal about how to resist from the way he resisted. We have one story of temptation he resisted just before his public ministry began. After fasting for forty days, the devil came personally and presented three temptations aimed right at Jesus' human weaknesses. The way Jesus resisted can teach us how to keep sin from "roosting" in our lives.

The First Temptation

Read Matthew 4:1-11.

Describe the circumstances surrounding Jesus' time of temptation. (Matthew 3:13-17)

> He was led into the wilderness by the Holy Spirit right after he was baptized by John.
>
> Note: Jesus had not yet begun his public ministry. Up until this point he was a relatively unknown carpenter.

What did Satan first tempt Jesus to do? (Matthew 4:3-4)

> To use his power to make bread so he could break his fast.

What would be tempting about suggesting that Jesus miraculously make bread?

> • Jesus was extremely hungry after fasting for 40 days.
>
> • Jesus had the power to do the miracle Satan suggested.

Why would it have been wrong for Jesus to give in to Satan's temptation?

> • He would have been using his power for personal gain.
>
> • He would not have been trusting the Father—his will or care for him.

How did Jesus respond? (Matthew 4:4)

> He quoted from God's Word: "It is written. . . ."

How can we imitate Jesus' example of resisting temptation here?

> We can memorize Scripture that corresponds directly to the area of temptation we're facing and apply it to that temptation.

The Second Temptation

What was the second temptation Jesus faced? (Matthew 4:5-7)

> To throw himself down from the top of the temple and have angels rescue him.

Why would it have been wrong for Jesus to give in to Satan's temptation?

> • It would have called into question God's promises—his word.
>
> • It would have been merely for show.

How did Jesus respond? (Matthew 4:7)

As before, he quoted Scripture.

The Third Temptation

What was the third temptation Satan tried on Jesus? (Matthew 4:8-10)

He offered to give Jesus rule of all the nations of the world.

What was the significance of this temptation?

It offered Jesus the rewards that the Father would give him after he died for our sins.

Note: This temptation had the biggest promise (all the kingdoms of the world) and the biggest price (worshipping the devil).

How did Jesus respond? (Matthew 4:10)

Once again, he quoted Scripture.

Note: If you leading a couples group, you may want to divide the group at this point. Have men get together in one part of the room and women in the other for the remainder of the discussion. The purpose here is to spend time sharing our temptations with one another for support, encouragement, and prayer. Report back to the whole group on the main points, but protect confidentiality by not specifying who said what.

What We Can Learn

Note: At this point you should reassemble the group to discuss these questions.

What do we learn about Satan's tactics from this story?

- He will misuse Scripture, lie, and bend the truth in order to deceive us—to get us to rationalize. He did this to Adam and Eve, he did it to Jesus, and he does it to us.

- He doesn't leave anybody alone. He even attacked the Son of God! Being spiritually mature, knowledgeable about the Bible, or sure of your faith doesn't mean you won't be tempted.

- One of his favorite tactics is to call into question our identity. As he whispered to Jesus, "If you're really the Son of God, then . . . ," he'll taunt us: "If you're really a child of God, how could you . . . ."

- He knows your weaknesses and will exploit them. First John 2:15-17 describes three main ones: (1) Lust of the flesh (desires for food, warmth, sex, sleep, comfort, and other physical pleasures); (2) lust of the eyes (desire for money, nice clothes, jewelry, cars, and other material things); (3) pride of life (desire for independence, status, power, position, and other signs of personal greatness).

He wanted Jesus to avoid the cross at all costs. Though we don't have the same cross as Jesus, we are told that we must die in order to live (Luke 9:23-24). Satan will seek to keep us from that "cross" as he tried to keep our Lord from his.

If you have time, ask:

How does Satan exploit the weaknesses mentioned in 1 John 2:15-17 in your life?

What can we learn about resisting temptation from Jesus' example?

- We *can* resist the devil. If we resist, he will eventually leave us alone.

- We need to know ourselves and our vulnerable areas so we can avoid situations that tempt us.

- We need to know the Scriptures well so we can spot misuses of the truth and thereby combat Satan's lies.

Note: The Bible is not a "magic charm" against the devil. Rather, it exposes his lies and robs them of their power.

BOTTOM LINE

Jesus is our example for how to respond to temptation.

YOUR WALK WITH GOD

Bible

Study Matthew 9 and 10 at least two times on each chapter.

Prayer

Day One: Adoration—Make a list of answers to this question: How has God shown his love for you recently? Praise God for each one.

Day Two: Confession—Paraphrase Psalm 51:1-4, putting it in words that speak directly to you, and use it as a guide for your prayer.

Day Three: Thanksgiving—Use Psalm 136 as a guide for your prayer.

Scripture Memory

No temptation has seized you except what is common to man. And God is faithful; he will not let you be tempted beyond what you can bear. But when you are tempted, he will also provide a way out so that you can stand up under it. 1 Corinthians 10:13

Next, we will take a look at the message of salvation that Jesus brought to the world. To prepare for the study, summarize in your own words what you would consider the main message of Jesus to be.

PRAYER

Have someone close the meeting in prayer.

The Message Jesus Brought

OVERVIEW

The purpose of this study is to help group members understand the basic salvation message.

Don't assume that everyone in your group already knows how to explain the gospel to others. For some it may have been a long time since they have had to verbalize it. Others might be familiar with it, but not know it well enough to explain it naturally in their own words.

PRAYER

Open the meeting in prayer.

REVIEW

Bible

Invite your group to share several observations and applications from Matthew 9 and 10.

Prayer

Adoration: Ask group members, **How has God shown his love for you recently?**

Confession: Invite a few volunteers to share their paraphrases of Psalm 51:1-4.

Thanksgiving: Ask the group how praying through Psalm 136 has affected their attitude in prayer.

Scripture Memory

See if everyone in your group can recite 1 Corinthians 10:13.

PURPOSE

It was many years ago, but you're sure you could get there again if you had to. You went to that quaint little restaurant on your honeymoon—how could you forget? And now you've just told a friend who's visiting the same area to be sure to go there. You've given him directions, confident your recollections accurately describe the way to get to the best seafood in town. Confident, that is, until you get a call from your friend because the roads don't go the way you recollected, and he went 45 minutes out of his way trusting in the map you drew from your memory. You hang up the phone wondering how you could have been so certain when you were so certainly wrong.

Many people think they have the facts straight about the Gospels and the identity of Jesus, but when they actually delve into message of the New Testament, they realize that several of their cherished ideas need serious revision. In the Gospel of John we encounter one such man who thought he understood God's ways but had to encounter the reality of his erroneous thinking. Nicodemus was not an atheist, but a religious teacher—someone familiar with God's revelation. In some ways, he was like many people today who are religious but misinformed—people who need the new birth from heaven brought by the Spirit. Jesus' statements to Nicodemus put the gospel message—the basic message of salvation—into a clear, concise package. We too should turn to this story as a model of how the gospel should be shared with others.

Jesus' Talk with Nicodemus

What do we know about Nicodemus? (John 3:1-2)

- He was a Jewish religious leader (a Pharisee).

- Well-educated (probably both the Scriptures and general knowledge).

- Older than Jesus.

- Probably wealthy (because of education and position).

How do we know that Nicodemus respected Jesus? (John 3:2)

He addressed Jesus as "Rabbi" and spoke of the miraculous workings as a sign of God's power.

Note: "Rabbi" means *teacher* and was a term of respect.

How did Jesus answer Nicodemus' words? (John 3:3)

He told him he needed to be born again.

Note: "Born again" means a new birth from the Spirit. We have all been born physically, but to be part of God's family we all need to be born again spiritually. This happens when we accept Jesus Christ's forgiveness by faith and acknowledge him as our leader for life. His Spirit intervenes and transforms us into a new creation.

What did Nicodemus misunderstand about Jesus' saying, "You must be born again"? (John 3:4)

He took Jesus literally and physically, when Jesus was talking about an inner transformation by the Spirit of God. Nicodemus knew about the concepts of trusting God by faith alone and being spiritually transformed (see Numbers 21:8-9; Jeremiah 31:33-34; and Ezekiel 36:26-27; 37:11-14), but apparently he had not connected it with salvation. He, like many of his peers, thought that salvation came by keeping the law. Nicodemus had substituted obeying the law and performing rituals for having a trust relationship with God.

Jesus' Talk with the Woman at the Well

What kind of person did Jesus meet? (John 4:4-8, 17-18)

A Samaritan woman who was living immorally.

How did Jesus answer the woman's question? (John 4:9-10)

He told her about living water.

What did Jesus want the woman to understand? (John 4:10-14, 25-26)

That salvation was available through him and that true spirituality was not a matter of "place" but of "condition."

If you have time, ask:

How would you contrast Nicodemus and the woman at the well? What significance do you attribute to the personal attention Jesus gave each of these very different people?

Nicodemus was an educated Jewish leader, outwardly righteous and respected among his people. The woman, in contrast, was an uneducated, immoral Samaritan woman. The two were different in almost every important way. This shows that Jesus did not discriminate between who could hear his message and who could not. He took his message of salvation to every kind of person.

Jesus' Main Message

How would you summarize Jesus' main message? (John 3:16; John 4:13-14)

We all need to be connected with God through faith. Trusting in his gift delivers religious people from the need to perform outward signs as a way of earning God's favor. To those who avoid or are afraid of religion, Jesus provides deliverance from their spiritual desert.

Note: The apostle Paul summarized this message in Ephesians 2:8-9. If you have time, read this passage together as a group and point out that, in both the Old and New Testaments, the object of faith has always been God. Faith—believing in, trusting in, and relying on God—has always been the means for appropriating God's gifts (for example: Genesis 15:6; Numbers 21:8-9; Isaiah 66:2; Galatians 3:6-11; Hebrews 11:1-3). Jesus' main message is that now he embodies the God we're to trust, and Paul underscores in the passage from Ephesians (and others) that we need to rely on God through faith.

BOTTOM LINE

Jesus' main message is that everybody needs salvation, and everybody needs to come by faith to him.

Bible

Study Matthew 11 three times, noting observations and applications.

Prayer

Day One: Adoration—How has God shown his patience to you recently? Thank him for his patience.

Day Two: Confession—Paraphrase Psalm 51:5-9 as you did with verses 1-4, and pray through it.

Day Three: Supplication—What are the three greatest needs in your life right now? Pray about those needs.

Scripture Memory

For God so loved the world that he gave his one and only Son, that whoever believes in him shall not perish but have eternal life. John 3:16

Next week we will study about those who followed Jesus—the disciples. What did Jesus want his disciples to be? What do you think Jesus expects out of a disciple today?

PRAYER

Have a group member close the meeting in prayer.

Jesus Selects His Team

The purpose of this study is to help group members see that Jesus calls us to follow him for life.

Many people don't know that Jesus had many more than just twelve disciples. They may also have some misconceptions about who the disciples were and what they did. This study can be an opportunity for you to challenge your group to be like one of the few who stuck with Jesus over the long haul.

PRAYER

Open the meeting in prayer by having everyone in the group say a short prayer of thanks for the work God has accomplished in the group.

REVIEW

Bible

Ask several volunteers to share their observations and applications from Matthew 11.

Prayer

Adoration: Ask group members, **How has God shown his patience to you recently?**

Confession: Have two or three members of your group share their paraphrases of Psalm 51:5-9.

Supplication: Ask the group, **What three needs did you pray about this week?**

Encourage everyone to write these down and to pray for one another during the coming week.

Scripture Memory

Have your group members recite John 3:16.

PURPOSE

The starting gun goes off. The crowd of runners surges forward. The spectators cheer. The TV cameras record the early leaders and the sports commentators tell us about those who have begun well.

But this is a *marathon,* not a sprint. Once the initial excitement of the start wears off, we become distracted by something else. Later in the day we'll turn back to see who wins. Only at the finish line will the thrill of the start be matched—and exceeded. What happens in between is usually of little interest to the spectators, yet that is where the race is won or lost.

The Christian life is like a marathon. Many enter and even start well. But it's hard to tell who's going to hang in there. Some get distracted or lack the endurance to finish. Others are deceived by their own confidence, tripping because they aren't cautious. Those who finish the race have disciplined their minds and bodies. They aren't sprinters, but long-distance runners. When the tedium and pain of the mid-race are almost unbearable, they persevere. They are the ones who finish well.

Jesus called the apostles to a marathon that we also know as discipleship. Some of them started well. Some of them tripped up along the way. One left the race—never to enter again. But Jesus wanted all of them to follow him—for the long haul.

The purpose of this study is to learn from the experience of the disciples that Jesus wants us to follow him for life.

Jesus' Disciples Then

What considerations did Jesus likely weigh when selecting the twelve apostles? (Luke 6:12-16)

In Jesus' early ministry, he attracted hundreds of followers. After he observed them for a while, he spent a night in prayer and then chose twelve to be apostles—twelve key people in whom he invested the majority of his time and attention. They would grow into the leaders who would carry on his ministry after his resurrection.

Note: Jesus made a distinction between apostles and disciples (Luke 6:13). What was the difference? "Disciple" means *learner, pupil;* thus, a disciple is anyone who follows Jesus. "Apostle" means *sent one, messenger;* the apostles were the small group of disciples whom Jesus hand-picked, called "the Twelve" at various places in the Gospels (Matthew 10:2-4; Mark 3:16-19; John 6:70).

Why is it significant that Jesus called the apostles to "be with him"? (Mark 3:14)

Jesus wanted the apostles to be with him so they could observe his life day in and day out. He wanted them to learn as an apprentice learns from a master, experiencing day-to-day activities together. Jesus wanted to model a lifestyle of love that they could imitate. He wanted them to know him thoroughly.

What happened to this group of twelve apostles by the time Jesus left earth? (Acts 1:21-26)

All but one (Judas) were still following Jesus.

Jesus' Disciples Today

What initially attracted you to Jesus—why did you become a Christian?

Have each person tell in two or three minutes how he or she came to faith in Christ.

Why do you still follow Jesus?

Have each person share his or her reasons.

Some disciples of Jesus stopped following him after a while (John 6:66-71). What causes Christians to give up following Christ?

Invite each person to respond. Come up with as many explanations as possible.

What are some of the benefits of staying faithful to Christ?

In addition to the answers your group members give, you can include these points as well:

- Answers the fundamental questions of life (Who am I? Why am I here? Where am I going?).

- Power for living (Jesus works on our behalf).

- Answered prayer (we go through life with a constant Companion).

- Fruit of obedience (destructive results of sin are minimized).

- Wisdom for today (written wisdom is in the Bible, although we need also to be aware of the prompting of the Holy Spirit).

Note: It is all too easy to take God for granted or to focus only on the costs of following Christ. We need to remind ourselves of the benefits too.

What motivates you to stay faithful to Jesus?

Invite each person to respond.

What do you need to do to be a better disciple?

Challenge every group member to make a public statement of what needs to be done to follow Christ better.

BOTTOM LINE

Jesus wants you to be one of his disciples for the long haul.

Bible

Study Matthew 12:1-21 three times, noting observations and applications.

Prayer

Day One: Adoration—How has God shown his grace (undeserved favor) to you recently? Thank him for his grace.

Day Two: Confession—Paraphrase Psalm 51:10-13 so that it reflects you and your circumstances, and use it as a guide for your prayer.

Day Three: Supplication—Identify some specific answers to prayer, as well as taking up some new requests.

Scripture Memory

Do you not know that in a race all the runners run, but only one gets the prize? Run in such a way as to get the prize.   1 Corinthians 9:24

To prepare for the next study, write down a wise saying or quote that provided direction or comfort in your life at some point.

PRAYER

Close the meeting with prayer.

8

The NewAttitudes

The purpose of this study is to help your group members understand the difference between the attitudes of the world and the attitudes of a true believer in Christ.

One way to help your group see clearly how to apply this portion of Scripture to life is to focus on how the Beatitudes contrast with the attitudes of the world. Emphasize this contrast as you lead the discussion.

PRAYER

Have a group member or two open the meeting with prayer.

REVIEW

Bible

Have your group share two observations and applications from Matthew 12:1-21.

Prayer

Adoration: Ask your group members, **What specific instances of God's grace did you note?**

Confession: Have volunteers read their paraphrases of Psalm 51:10-13. Ask how it helped them.

Requests: Ask your group members what specific answers to prayer they have seen recently.

Scripture Memory

See how many in your group can recite 1 Corinthians 9:24.

PURPOSE

What would you do if you were turned down for a lucrative job after weeks of grueling interviews? Would you sit back, become depressed, and blame yourself for not being a more dynamic person? Or would you take the setback in stride and look forward to the next opportunity? It all depends on your *attitude*. The attitudes that shape our actions often go a long way in determining the quality of our friendships, the performance of our jobs, and our service for God. In a very real way, attitude is everything.

Attitude is the central theme of one of the most famous passages in all of Scripture: the Sermon on the Mount found in Matthew 5–7. The Sermon on the Mount is central to Jesus' teaching, summarizing the characteristics of those who know God personally. Here Jesus instructs us on how we ought to live and who we ought to be. It is a message Jesus gave repeatedly as he traveled from place to place.

This is the first of two studies on the Sermon on the Mount. This study covers Matthew 5:1-16, the section in which Jesus describes believers' NewAttitudes or "Beatitudes," as they're often called. We will learn several ways in which Jesus wants our attitudes and actions to be different from the world's.

Have your group members turn to Matthew 5.

The Beatitudes

What does it mean to be poor in spirit? (Matthew 5:3)

- Be humble.

- Depend on God.

What should we mourn over? (Matthew 5:4)

- Sin.

- The consequences of evil.

What does it mean to be meek? (Matthew 5:5)

Gentle.

Why is it important for us to desire righteousness? (Matthew 5:6)

It is the first step in becoming righteous.

Why is it important to show mercy to others? (Matthew 5:7)

The merciful are the ones who receive mercy.

What is purity in heart? (Matthew 5:8)

Integrity.

What does it mean to be a "peacemaker"? (Matthew 5:9)

- To help others become reconciled.

- To practice fairness.

- To break down walls between others.

- To refuse to fight over unimportant matters when provoked.

Why are righteous people sometimes persecuted? (Matthew 5:10-12)

They convict others of their unrighteousness. Those who persecute them are rejecting Christ and all he stands for.

The Beatitudes vs. the World's Attitudes

Fill in the blanks from your experience:

Answers may vary. We've included some suggested contrasting ideas.

Jesus Says

Blessed are the poor in spirit

Blessed are those who mourn

Blessed are the meek

Blessed are those who hunger
and thirst for righteousness

Blessed are the merciful

Blessed are the pure in heart

Blessed are the peacemakers

Blessed are those who are
persecuted because of
righteousness

The World Says

Blessed are the aggressive

Blessed are the tough

Blessed are the powerful

Blessed are the self-fulfilled

Blessed are the hard-hearted

Blessed are the manipulators

Blessed are those who get
results at all costs

Blessed are those who don't
make waves

Which of these attitudes do you find most difficult to live out? Why?

Share a personal example to get the discussion started.

Knowing that Jesus wants you to display eventually all of these attitudes, where do you think he would want you to start this week?

Encourage volunteers to reply, but don't put anyone on the spot.

What steps can you take to live out these NewAttitudes?

Answers may include: confess sin that is holding us back, find a person to hold us accountable for behavior we need to change, spend more time in prayer, and so on.

BOTTOM LINE

**The attitudes God wants us to have are radically
different from the attitudes of the world.**

Bible

Study Matthew 12:22-50 during your three appointments with God.

Prayer

Day One: Adoration—In what recent situation have you clearly seen God's wisdom?

Day Two: Confession—Paraphrase Psalm 51:14-19, applying it to your own struggle with sin, and use it as a guide for prayer.

Day Three: Thanksgiving—List five things related to your family for which you are thankful.

Scripture Memory

Review the following verses: 1 Corinthians 10:13; John 3:16; and 1 Corinthians 9:24.

Next week we will continue our study of the Sermon on the Mount. Take some time to consider your motives for your behavior? Why is it so difficult to have pure motives?

PRAYER

Close the meeting with prayer.

The Power of Pure Motives

The purpose of this study is to help your group members learn the importance of thoughts, attitudes, and motives in obeying God.

Everyone finds it easier to do good outwardly than to have pure thoughts and motives, so this study should hit home. As you deal with each topic, talk about specific areas in which you and your group members need to make adjustments.

PRAYER

Open the meeting with prayer.

REVIEW

Bible

Invite volunteers to share their observations and applications from Matthew 12:22-50. Also ask what sort of questions the passage raised in their minds and what answers they were able to find.

Prayer

Adoration: Have your group share ways God has given them wisdom recently.

Confession: Have volunteers read their paraphrases of Psalm 51:14-19. Then ask:

What benefits have you gained from paraphrasing this Psalm over the last several weeks?

Scripture Memory

Have your group members recite 1 Corinthians 10:13, John 3:16, and 1 Corinthians 9:24.

PURPOSE

It is easy to judge people by what you see. Want to know who's the most committed to the church? Just look at who arrives on Sunday morning first and stays the longest. Want to know who reads God's Word faithfully? Just look at the person who brings a well-worn Bible to small group. It is tempting to measure each other by what we see outwardly. It is also easy to judge motives unfairly. In particular, we tend to believe that our motives are pure and suspect the motives of others.

God is as concerned with your motives as he is with your outward behavior. He cares about why and how you give, not just how much. He is concerned with why you do good, not just that you do it. Outward obedience alone does not impress God. He wants your heart. In this study, you will explore the importance of your motives in all you do.

STUDY

The Power of Pure Motives

How do inner attitudes and thoughts affect our outward behavior?

Be prepared with a personal example if discussion is slow.

Why is it difficult to do good deeds in secret?

> We love recognition, and there is no immediate payoff for doing good in secret.

Motives to Watch

1 Murder

What inner feelings or attitudes are identified with the outward behavior of murder? (Matthew 5:21-26)

> Anger, contempt, hatred.

2 Adultery

Why did Jesus go beyond condemning the act of adultery? (Matthew 5:27-28)

> Many people harbor lustful thoughts but don't carry them out because they fear being found out. Jesus is saying that these lustful attitudes are just as bad as actually committing adultery.

Why do you think Jesus used such violent imagery to describe how we should resist sin? (Matthew 5:29-30)

> He wants us to take drastic measures to resist sin. He obviously didn't intend for us to take these words literally—maimed people still sin if their *hearts* haven't been changed.

3 Hatred

What inner attitude toward enemies did Jesus condemn? (Matthew 5:43-44)

> Hatred, contempt.

How do we combat the tendency to scorn our enemies? (Matthew 5:43-44)

> Love them; treat them well; help them.

4 Giving

What do we need to watch out for in doing good? (Matthew 6:1)

> The motive of doing good merely for show or to gain recognition from others.

How should we give? (Matthew 6:2-4)

> So that others don't know what we're doing.

5 Praying

How would you describe prayer that is pleasing to God? (Matthew 6:5-8)

> • In secret.

- To communicate to God, not to impress people.

- Meaningfully, not with meaningless repetition.

6 Fasting

In what way should we fast? (Matthew 6:16-18)

- In secret.

- With concern for God's favor, not other people's sympathy and admiration.

7 Storing up Treasures

What is a spiritual attitude toward material things?

- The most significant investments are eternal, not material.

- Material things don't last.

- What you value will become your passion.

- You cannot live for both things and God.

8 Worry

Why is it harmful to worry about having enough material things? (Matthew 6:25-34)

- It shows concern for things above serving God.

- It doesn't do any good.

- It is a poor use of time and energy.

- It denies the fact that God can meet your needs.

As you look over this study, what motives do you recognize that hinder your relationship with God? (Matthew 6:25-34)

Give a personal example here.

What steps could you take to bring your inner self more in line with God's desire for you?

Confess sin, renew your mind according to God's Word, pray with others, find an accountability partner, and so on.

BOTTOM LINE

God is as concerned about your motives as he is about your behavior.

Bible

Study Matthew 13 three times. Focus on the Parable of the Seeds.

Prayer

Day One: Adoration—Go for a walk. Carry on a simple conversation with God that includes elements of adoration, confession, thanksgiving, and supplication. Try talking softly out loud as you walk.

Day Two: Supplication—Say something or do something to encourage someone else. You could write a note, make a phone call, buy a small gift, or make something. Then pray specifically for that person.

Day Three: Confession—Take an inventory of your life. Claim God's forgiveness for any sin you recall. Also respond to the following two questions:

- What do you need God's power for this week?
- What do you need God's wisdom for this week?

Scripture Memory

But the LORD said to Samuel, "Do not consider his appearance or his height, for I have rejected him. The LORD does not look at the things man looks at. Man looks at the outward appearance, but the LORD looks at the heart."   1 Samuel 16:7

Next week we will explore some of the parables that Jesus spoke. Why do you think Jesus told so many parables when he could have simply explained the principles he wanted to communicate?

Close the meeting in prayer.

He Spoke in Parables

OVERVIEW

The purpose of this study is to help group members understand the significance of Jesus' use of parables and grasp the main point of several of them.

As your group members discuss the points in this study, watch out for the hazard of over-analyzing each parable. Like any illustration, parables are not perfect analogies. They do not necessarily have lessons hidden in every minute detail. Rather, these stories usually communicate one essential point. When studying parables, keep in mind the old adage: don't miss the forest for the trees!

PRAYER

Open the meeting with prayer.

REVIEW

Bible

Ask: **What observations and applications did you make from Matthew 13?**

Prayer

Ask these questions to find out how everyone did with their appointments with God:

How did it go praying during your walk this week?

What did you do to encourage someone?

Scripture Memory

Encourage everyone to recite 1 Samuel 16:7.

PURPOSE

A mother sits in a rocking chair, holding a child in her lap and a book so that the child can see. As she reads, the child listens in rapt attention. Perhaps you remember having stories read to you. If so, you can probably also remember many details of the stories you heard. Stories have a way of sticking with us over the years.

Pastors also always use stories in the form of illustrations in their sermons. You probably can remember a story your pastor told last week more readily than you can remember his main points. That's because our minds retain pictures more easily than words.

Jesus told many stories. He took common, ordinary experiences and used them to explain spiritual truths that he wanted his disciples to put into practice. We call these stories parables. Altogether the Gospels contain 32 different parables. This is an important part of what Jesus taught. If we are to learn from Jesus, we must become students of his parables.

This study highlights eight of Jesus' parables, all from Matthew 13. You will examine them closely to learn how to learn from a parable.

The Sower and the Seed

What is the main point of this parable? (Matthew 13:1-23)

People respond in a variety of ways to the Word of God; only one produces the change that God seeks. Be careful what you do after hearing the Word of God.

Was there a time in your life when your "soil" was not ready to receive God's Word?

Give a personal example.

The Tares among the Wheat

What lesson did Jesus want to communicate in comparing people to tares and wheat? (Matthew 13:24-30, 36-43)

We have to tolerate evil for now, but a day is coming when it will be dealt with once and for all. God will judge the unrighteous and reward his children, even though today they may sit side by side in church!

The Mustard Seed

Why did Jesus choose the mustard seed to illustrate faith? (Matthew 13:31-32)

Something that begins small and insignificant can eventually grow to become predominant—like God's work, which starts small but grows.

Note: The mustard seed was indeed among the tiniest known in the Middle East and came to be associated in various ways with small things. A mustard tree could grow to as large as 15 feet high.

The Leaven

What qualities does yeast possess that would make it a fitting illustration of the kingdom of heaven? (Matthew 13:33)

The same as that about the mustard seed: Something that begins small and insignificant, like God's work, can eventually have far reaching influence.

The Hidden Treasure

What is the main point of this parable? (Matthew 13:44)

When someone finds a great treasure, he or she will spare no expense to obtain it. The wealth and joy that comes from finding Christ ought to make us willing to sacrifice anything to be completely his.

The Costly Pearl

Why is a pearl of great value like the kingdom of heaven? (Matthew 13:45-46)

Such a pearl would be the find of a lifetime and a cause for rejoicing after a long search. In the same way the gospel is more valuable than anything else. We can't give up more than we get when we embrace Jesus and his kingdom.

Note: Jesus wasn't saying that we can buy our way into heaven; he was merely illustrating the priceless value of salvation. (Compare Proverbs 3:14-15.)

The Fishing Net

Why would Jesus compare a fishing net to the kingdom of heaven? (Matthew 13:47-50)

A fishing net catches everything in its trail. And at the end of age, all people, saved and unsaved, will be gathered together and judged. Though evil and good coexist, even in good places, a time is coming when God will sort out and deal with false believers as well as nonbelievers from among his people.

The Unmerciful Servant

What is the main point of this parable? (Matthew 18:21-35)

We have wronged and offended God, yet he willingly forgave us. We should imitate him and forgive those who wrong us as well.

Why do you think Jesus used so many parables in his teaching? (Matthew 13:1-23)

These stories were memorable for their vivid images and important lessons. Jesus undoubtedly used them because they would stick with their listeners longer than abstract ideas.

Which of the above parables relates to a concern you have for someone else? Explain your answer.

YOUR WALK WITH GOD

Bible

Read Matthew 14 three times, noting observations and applications.

Prayer

Day One: Adoration—Listen to one side of a praise tape in an undistracted, quiet atmosphere.

Day Two: Confession—Call someone in the group and ask him or her to pray for you concerning a temptation you face. Pray together on the phone or at some other time.

Day Three: Supplication—Pray specifically for one aspect of the ministry of your church.

Scripture Memory

But seek first his kingdom and his righteousness, and all these things will be given to you as well.   Matthew 6:33

Next week we will take a closer look at the compassion that Jesus demonstrated for people. Why do some people think that God lacks compassion?

PRAYER

Have someone close the meeting in prayer.

213

Jesus—A Man of Compassion

OVERVIEW

The purpose of this study is to help group members understand the compassion that Jesus has for the world.

The people in your group will have differing reactions to this study. Some already think of Jesus as compassionate, and will have no problem with the concepts. Some may know that he is compassionate, yet for a variety of reasons their feelings lag well behind their understanding. Still others may find it impossible to believe that *anyone* could have compassion on them, least of all someone they can't see. As you lead, be sensitive to the differences in your group in the way people identify with our compassionate Lord.

PRAYER

Open the meeting with prayer.

Bible

Invite your group to discuss their observations and applications of Matthew 14.

Prayer

Ask:

What was your reaction to listening to a worship tape?

For what ministries of our church did you pray?

Scripture Memory

Invite everyone to recite Matthew 6:33.

PURPOSE

"You say that God loves the world, but I don't feel it."

"God is out there and I am here, what does it mean to say I matter to him?"

"Jesus could never love me after the things I've done."

Most people have trouble feeling God's love. Some just don't feel much of anything, so God's love seems meaningless to them. Some are pressed down under the weight of their failures and feel too ashamed and unworthy to embrace God's care. It's difficult to grow in a relationship with God without becoming aware of and accepting his compassion for us. Yet when we understand the depth of God's great tenderness toward us, we are better able to love him back in response.

The purpose of this study is to help you understand the compassionate side of Jesus. You'll learn that Jesus wants to show compassion to those in need—including you.

Jesus and the Death of Lazarus

What was Jesus' response to the news of Lazarus' death? (John 11:33-38)

> His heart was broken as our hearts are with the loss of a loved one. Note that Jesus wept openly.

Can you relate to Jesus' feelings here?

> Mention a personal example if appropriate.

What does this tell you about Jesus?

> • He was able to hurt for people.
>
> • He was able to grieve.
>
> • He experienced deep emotions as we do.

Jesus and the Multitudes

What does Jesus' response to the death of John the Baptist tell you about how he was feeling?

> He needed time to be alone and grieve, as all of us do when we experience deep personal loss.

When Jesus saw the large crowd that had gathered to see him, how did he view the interruption on his attempt to get away? (Matthew 14:13-14)

> He had compassion on them in spite of his personal grief.

How would you describe the disciples' attitude toward the crowd? (Matthew 14:15)

> They suggested that the crowd be sent away, perhaps demonstrating their impatience and lack of compassion for their needs.

Jesus and You

Tell about a time that someone showed compassion toward you. What kind of impact did this have on you?

> It's important that everyone try to identify a time they received compassion.

Read Matthew 11:28-30. What is one way Jesus demonstrates his compassion? Explain how this compassion is manifested practically in a Christian's life.

He offers to take our burdens. This relief could be initiated through a change in circumstances Jesus initiates, or more probably through an inner peace and ability to cope with the difficulties.

What makes it easy or difficult for you to see Jesus as compassionate?

Invite everyone to respond.

In what way has Jesus' compassion touched your life in a way you can feel?

Invite everyone to respond.

Jesus and Your World

Why do people sometimes find it hard to believe that God loves them?

Probably because they've never experienced unconditional love and so feel unworthy.

In what settings are you able to share Christ's compassion with others?

Invite everyone to respond with the opportunities they see around them.

What can you do this week to show Christ's compassion to another person in need?

If group members have a difficult time thinking of a personal application, remind them of the verse about the "least of these" (Matthew 25:40).

BOTTOM LINE

Jesus' compassion, like every other
part of his character, is perfect.

YOUR WALK WITH GOD

Bible

Read Matthew 15 three times, noting observations and applications.

Prayer

Day One: Adoration—List attributes of God that you think of easily when observing or enjoying creation.

Day Two: Confession—Go for a walk and use it as a time to "clear the air" between you and the Lord. Be thorough, and claim his complete forgiveness.

Day Three: Thanksgiving—Fill in the following blanks, thanking God for . . .

A spiritual blessing:

A friendship blessing:

A family blessing:

A spouse or relational blessing:

A material blessing:

Scripture Memory

Come to me, all you who are weary and burdened, and I will give you rest.   Matthew 11:28

Next week we will take a closer look at the times when Jesus healed those who were sick. What difference do you think it made that Jesus could heal those who were sick? Do you think God still heals people in our day?

PRAYER

Close the meeting in prayer.

Jesus the Healer

OVERVIEW

The purpose of this study is to help your group members understand the compassion of Jesus and have confidence in his power to help in times of need.

This study, like the last one, emphasizes the compassion that Jesus had on people in need. He didn't limit his ministry to people's souls, but was concerned for bodies and emotions as well.

Some discussion may arise as to how God heals people today. Be careful to avoid unhelpful tangents and divisive arguments about whether or not miraculous healings should always happen in our day. The point is that Jesus did heal people and that this truth can increase our confidence that he cares for all we are and all we need.

PRAYER

Open the meeting with prayer.

REVIEW

Bible

Have group members share their observations and applications from Matthew 15.

Prayer

Have group members tell what attributes of God were brought to mind by their thoughts on creation.

Find out what everyone thought of their "confession walk." Ask: **What was helpful about your walk?**

Also ask: **For what blessings in your list did you thank God?**

Scripture Memory

Invite everyone to recite Matthew 11:28.

PURPOSE

If you moved to a new city, how would you choose your family physician? Chances are you would take into consideration a number of important qualifications. Certainly you would want someone who was knowledgeable and who kept up with the rapid changes in medicine. Just as important, however, would be that doctor's concern for your entire well being. You would want to sense that this physician genuinely cared about *you* and would want to do everything in his or her power to keep you well or help you get over an illness.

Jesus' healing ministry was a highly personal part of his work. Lest we imagine huge crowds gathered to watch him perform these great miracles, we should keep in mind that he taught the masses, but healed individuals. Even when others were looking, he performed healings by touching each person one by one. (The only exception was when he healed ten lepers as a group, but even then they were apart from the crowd.) Remember that one of Satan's temptations was to lure Jesus into using his power to razzle-dazzle potential followers (Matthew 4:5-6). Jesus did not use his healing power to draw crowds. He healed people to substantiate his claims and to demonstrate his compassion. He wanted people to be healed, and he also wanted them to understand that he was the one they were waiting for—the Messiah.

This study will show you that Jesus did indeed heal those who were sick. You can have confidence in his compassion and his power to help you in times of need.

Healing the Centurion's Servant

What facts do you observe about the centurion? (Luke 7:1-10)

- He cared deeply for his servant.

- He had heard about Jesus.

- He was humble—sent a delegation because he didn't consider himself worthy of Jesus' personal attention.

- He had good relationship with the Jewish elders—unusual for a military commander of the occupying forces.

- He had built and paid for a synagogue.

- He had respect for Jesus.

- He had faith in Jesus' power and authority, even over creation.

- He astonished Jesus with his faith.

What can this story teach us about asking Jesus to heal others? (Luke 7:1-10)

- God listens when we ask him to heal others.

- God responds to faith.

Raising the Widow's Son

What strikes you about the healing of the widow's son? (Luke 7:11-17)

- The boy was the woman's only child.

- Jesus was moved by the woman's sorrow.

- Jesus healed the boy even before the woman asked him to.

- Jesus touched the coffin—a violation of Jewish tradition.

- Jesus led the healed boy back to his mother.

Note: A widow often had low social status in that culture.

What does this story teach us about Jesus?

- He cares deeply about hurting people.

- Sometimes he meets our needs even before we ask him.

Raising Jairus' Daughter

Who was Jairus? (Mark 5:21-43)

>   ➤ He was a synagogue official.

>   ➤ He knew Jesus could heal his daughter.

>   ➤ He did *not* know that Jesus could raise his daughter back to life.

What can this story teach us about trusting God?

We should not lose faith in his desire to help, because God is able to act even when we think all hope is lost.

Healing of the Hemorrhaging Woman

What impresses you about the woman Jesus healed? (Mark 5:24-34)

>   ➤ She believed Jesus could heal her.

>   ➤ She was healed.

What can this story teach us about asking Jesus for help?

Jesus wants to hear our requests, and responds when we reach out to him.

Healing of Ten Lepers

What are some significant details in this healing? (Luke 17:11-19)

>   ➤ The whole group stood at a distance, but all wanted to be healed.

>   ➤ All ten were healed, but only after they obeyed Christ and left.

>   ➤ Only one, a Samaritan, came back to thank Jesus.

Note: Standing at a distance was required by law because of their leprosy. Also, Samaritans were non-Jews who shared some roots with the Jewish people but had different religious traditions. They were generally scorned by the Jews in Jesus' day.

What can this story teach us about expecting to see results from our prayers?

>   ➤ Sometimes we must take a step of obedience before we see any change.

>   ➤ God deserves our thanks when circumstances turn our way.

Conclusion

What general observation can you make from the healings studied here?

> See what other insights or applications emerge.

What do these healings show us about the nature of Jesus?

> - He is compassionate, he cares for us when we hurt.
> - God wants us to turn to him when we feel hopeless.
> - Without faith, it is impossible to please God.
> - When we demonstrate faith, God is pleased to act.
> - The one we trust in, Jesus, is compassionate.
> - God wants to hear us say thanks.

How do we know it's worthwhile to pray about physical and emotional needs in our life?

> Jesus cares about us, and he demonstrated his willingness and ability to help.

BOTTOM LINE

You can pray to Jesus with
confidence in times of need.

YOUR WALK WITH GOD

Bible

Read Psalm 23 three times. Also, review the application questions in On Your Own.

Prayer

Day One: Adoration—Write down your thoughts to this question: What does the sending of Jesus tell you about God? Spend some time praising him for what you found.

Day Two: Confession—Think back over the events and conversations of this week. For what do you need to claim God's forgiveness?

Day Three: Thanksgiving—List three positive values you picked up from your family. Thank God for them, and then tell your parents or your siblings your thoughts if possible.

Scripture Memory

Review the following verses: 1 Samuel 16:7; Matthew 6:33; and Matthew 11:28.

Next week we will review the main lessons learned in *The Incomparable Jesus.* What have you learned about Jesus? What other insights have been helpful?

PRAYER

Close the meeting with prayer.

ON YOUR OWN

Questions for Application

One reason why some Christians find Bible study lifeless and routine is that they fail to apply the passages they've read to their lives. Many times the solution to this problem is to develop a regular habit of asking questions that will help you personalize the Scripture message you've read. We've drawn up a list of questions you can use. Try them this week as you are reading your Bible assignment.

Is there a promise to claim?

(Hebrews 13:5)

Is there a command to obey?

(Ephesians 5:21)

Is there sin to confess?

(1 Corinthians 6)

Is there an example to follow?

(1 Thessalonians 2:5)

Is there a behavior to change?

(Ephesians 4:25ff)

Is there an encouragement to receive?

(Philippians 4:13)

Is there an insight to gain?

(Romans 8:28)

Is there an issue to pray about?

(1 Timothy 2:3-4)

Is there a reason to worship God?

(Romans 11:33-36)

Reviewing The Incomparable Jesus

The purpose of this study is to help group members assess what they've learned about Jesus.

The final unit of this study guide will give your group members an opportunity to review what they've learned in this study guide.

Bible

Have the group share observations and applications from Psalm 23.

Prayer

Adoration: Ask group members, **What does the sending of Jesus tell you about God the Father?**

Thanksgiving: Ask group members to identify a couple of positive values they picked up from their families.

Scripture Memory

Have group members recite the following verses: 1 Samuel 16:7; Matthew 6:33; and Matthew 11:28.

PURPOSE

This review culminates your study of *The Incomparable Jesus,* the second book in the *Walking With God Series.* Use this time to reflect on your experience and summarize what you've learned about Christ. It can also be an affirming time to express your appreciation to fellow group members for the growing bond between you.

Being a Christian means more than just knowing about Jesus; it means knowing him personally. Our knowledge of Christ should change us. As you do this review, spend time sharing how Jesus is changing you.

STUDY

Discoveries about Jesus

Why is it significant that Jesus fulfilled the prophecies of the Old Testament?

This shows he truly was the Messiah, not just a man, a prophet, or a person pretending to be God.

Why is it important to affirm that Jesus was both fully God and fully man?

Our salvation depends on knowing who Jesus really is (John 8:24).

Note: Cults always deny some aspect of who Jesus is.

What do we learn about resisting temptation from Jesus resisting Satan in the wilderness?

We learn that it is important to use Scripture, be prepared, and be encouraged that we too can resist temptation.

What do we learn about ministering to others from the way Jesus selected and nurtured his twelve apostles?

> He made his selection carefully and built the apostles up over time by challenging them and sharing experiences with them.

How would you summarize Jesus' main message (the gospel)?

> Refer to John 3:16 or Ephesians 2:8-9.

Which of the Beatitudes do you find to be the most challenging to apply?

> Give a personal example.

Why does religious behavior without the proper motives fail to please God?

> Refer to 1 Samuel 16:7.

How do we know that Jesus has compassion on us?

> He demonstrated it in his healing and teaching while he was here on earth.

What are some biblical examples of Jesus showing concern for individual people?

> Any of the stories of Jesus healing would suffice.

Discoveries about Yourself

During the past twelve weeks, how have you grown in your relationship with Jesus?

Name two or three specific ways you are trying to be different as a result of this study.

In what ways has this study of the incomparable Jesus affected your attitudes?

YOUR WALK WITH GOD

Bible

You are free to study any passage, chapter, or book of the Bible this week, but be prepared to discuss any observations or applications you noted.

Prayer

Pray that you'll come to know Christ more deeply.

Scripture Memory

Review the following verses: Matthew 26:41; Philippians 2:5-7; Hebrews 1:1-2; 1 Corinthians 10:13; John 3:16; 1 Corinthians 9:24; 1 Samuel 16:7; Matthew 6:33; Matthew 11:28.

PRAYER

You or any member of the group should close in prayer.

Arrange a time to sit down with each group member individually over the next few weeks. (If your group is a couples group, have men meet with men, women with women, or couples with couples.) Have them discuss their perspectives on their spiritual growth as measured by the four categories listed above.

Self-Evaluation

Your group leader will be meeting with you to discuss your current spiritual condition and your hopes for growing in your faith. Please take some time to reflect honestly on where you stand right now within these four basic categories of Christian growth. Rate yourself in each category.

+   **Doing well. I'm pleased with my progress so far.**

✓   **On the right track, but I see definite areas for improvement.**

—   **This is a struggle. I need some help.**

A Disciple Is One Who . . .

Walks with God

To what extent is my Bible study and prayer time adequate for helping me walk with God?

Rating:

Comments:

Lives the Word

To what extent is my mind filled with scriptural truths so that my actions and reactions show I am being transformed?

Rating:

Comments:

Contributes to the work

To what extent am I actively participating in the church with my time, talents, and treasures?

Rating:

Comments:

Impacts the world

To what extent am I impacting my world with a Christian witness and influence?

Rating:

Comments:

Other issues I would kike to discuss with my small group leader:

"Follow Me!"

Walking With Jesus in Everyday Life

Introduction

Salvation is described by the Scriptures as a free gift. Yet Jesus also spoke of discipleship as costly, and urged those who would follow him to count the cost. For Jesus, no final conflict existed between receiving his gracious forgiveness and following his exacting lordship. He knew that as Savior he was offering something to sinful people that they couldn't earn, yet as their Lord he was calling them to a life of service which required obedience at every turn. The concept of receiving the gift without deference to the Giver was unthinkable.

To take part in the relationship ("Savior" and "Forgiver") without embracing *all* Jesus is ("Master" and "Leader") would be as ridiculous as going through a marriage ceremony without anticipating a lifetime of loving and serving your spouse. Technically, you don't become married just by acting like you're married, and you don't become a Christian by living a good life, but would it make any sense to become married with no intention of acting like it? Does it make sense to receive Christ without responding daily in obedience to his commands?

Ephesians 2:8-9 promises us unconditional grace that saves us; the very next verse (2:10) tells us that God prepared good works for us to walk in them. In this book, we will examine in greater detail what it means to follow Christ as Lord day by day. This will bring you and your group members to a point where you can identify areas for personal growth and what, in particular, what you need to do to make the lordship of Christ more functional in your lives.

Follow Me . . . I'll Protect You

OVERVIEW

The purpose of this study is to help your group members understand the significance of obeying God and his Word.

This is the first of two studies on the subject of obedience. Studying this topic will benefit everyone in your group because all of us struggle with doing what is right. The commands may be spelled out for us clearly enough in the Bible, yet clarity is often not the problem. *Doing* what is right is usually more difficult than *knowing* what is.

Your group members need to know the difference between true obedience to Christ and mere conformity. Jesus is just as concerned about what is in the hearts of his followers as he is about their outward actions.

The rest of the material in this study guide about Jesus will be more meaningful if we first clarify the significance of obeying Christ. Then we will learn so that we can walk more like him and not simply learn so that we can talk more about him.

PRAYER

Begin the meeting with a short prayer. This is what you should do first each week after everybody has arrived. It marks the formal beginning of every meeting.

Invite God to lead your time together and that his Spirit would move freely among you.

To build rapport, begin the meeting with the following question.

Can you recall a humorous incident from your childhood where you got into trouble for disobeying? Describe the circumstances.

If your group is continuing from the second study guide in this series, *The Incomparable Jesus,* use this review. Otherwise, skip ahead to Purpose.

Bible

Have your group members share their observations and applications from the Bible passages they selected and studied since the last meeting.

Prayer

Invite group members to share how prayer has helped them get to know Jesus better.

Scripture Memory

See if your group can recite all of the memory verses from *The Incomparable Jesus:* Matthew 26:41; Philippians 2:5-7; Hebrews 1:1-2; 1 Corinthians 10:13; John 3:16; 1 Corinthians 9:24; 1 Samuel 16:7; Matthew 6:33; Matthew 11:28.

Have your group members open their books to the first study. Then read this introduction, or have one of the group members read it while the others follow along.

A small child was once asked to sit down in the car. "I can't drive until you sit and buckle your seat belt," said the mother.

"No," replied the child.

"I will tell you again—sit down and buckle your belt."

"No," was the defiant answer.

"You either sit down and obey me, or we'll both get out of the car and I'll spank you!" responded the exasperated mother.

The child just glared at her silently. As the mother began to open the car door to make good on her threat, the child immediately sat down and buckled the belt.

"That's better," said the mother.

As they began to drive off, the child said under his breath but loud enough to be heard, "I may be sitting down on the outside, but I'm standing up on the inside."

This story illustrates several important concepts about obedience. First, obedience maintains interpersonal harmony, while its opposite—disobedience—causes conflicts. When someone disobeys an authority, friction occurs between the two. Second, when the person issuing directives does the right thing, obedience is for our well-being. Third, obedience is not the same as mere conformity to someone else's wishes. How often are we "standing up on the inside" even though we're "sitting down on the outside!" True obedience is done willingly out of trust in the one with authority; conformity is merely begrudging adjustment of our outward actions.

In this study we will explore what it means to obey Christ.

What Is Obedience?

What does it mean to have authority?

To have the right to tell someone else what to do; to have the right to command.

In what ways do you respond or have you responded to the authority of:

the government?

a parent?

a coach?

the church?

What does it mean in practical (rather than theological) terms to call Jesus "Lord"? (Luke 6:46)

> It means to do what he says; to obey him.

What does our level of obedience to God show us? (John 14:15)

> How much we do or don't love and trust God.

Who does Jesus say are his "brothers and sisters"? (Matthew 12:47-50)

> Those who obey God.

Why Is Obedience to God So Important?

> This set of questions is the heart of the study. Have someone look up each verse and read it to the rest of the group before you discuss the questions.

What effect does our obedience have on God? (1 Thessalonians 4:1-2)

> It pleases him.

In what ways does obedience protect us?

> Psalm 32:3-7
>
> > God protects us from trouble.
>
> Psalm 119:45
>
> > We have freedom—security—within the boundaries of God's law.
>
> Romans 1:27
>
> > Obedience protects us from the consequences of sin.

How has obedience to God protected you?

> Encourage everyone to share. Be prepared with an example from your own life.

What effect does obedience and disobedience have on our conscience?

Ephesians 4:18-19

Repeated disobedience to God hardens us toward doing wrong.

1 Timothy 1:19

Obeying God gives us a clear conscience.

1 Timothy 4:2

A seared conscience leads a person to sin shamelessly.

How has God's Word influenced your behavior in an area that otherwise probably wouldn't matter to you?

Be prepared with a personal example if discussion starts slowly.

According to the following verses, what different effects can obedience to God have on our relationships with others?

Luke 6:22-23

Some people are turned away by our actions and life-style.

Luke 6:27-28

We become more loving and helpful to others, even enemies.

When has your obedience to God negatively impacted a personal relationship?

Some may mention friends who have been put off by their faith. Allow each person an opportunity to answer.

When have you chosen to respond with kindness toward someone who has mistreated you for being a Christian?

Again, give each person an opportunity to answer.

BOTTOM LINE

Following Jesus means obeying him.

At the end of every study is a section called "The Bottom Line." Each week you should read this summary sentence and have your group members write it down in their study guide word for word.

Make sure your group understands the assignment for next week.

Bible

Schedule three times this week to get alone with God. Pick times during the day that work best for you. Each time, read 1 Peter 1, noting observations and applications.

Prayer

Day One: Adoration—List ten ways God has shown his faithfulness to you.

Day Two: Confession—Review the last two days and write out a prayer of confession.

Day Three: Thanksgiving—Give thanks to God for three qualities in your spouse or a close friend. Then tell that person about what you were thankful for.

Scripture Memory

As part of the curriculum, we've included memory verses with each study. If you want to make this discipline part of your discipleship experience, begin by memorizing this verse:

Why do you call me, "Lord, Lord," and do not do what I say?   Luke 6:46

> The assignment at the end of each study is designed to be done during the group members' quiet time. In fact, *their homework is a quiet time.* Whatever else this small group experience does for your group members, it will help them establish a habit of regular appointments with God.
>
> To assist group members in organizing their homework, we've prepared the spiritual journey notebook called The *Walking With God Journal.* This journal includes instructions for how to have a quiet time and blank pages to write out their Bible study notes and prayers. Your group members may find this study tool useful as they meet with God each week.

Next week we will explore what it means to obey Christ in the "gray areas" of life. To prepare for the study, think about how you determine what is right and wrong for you when there are no specific commands about the issue in

Scripture. What principles have you found useful for making decisions in these situations?

Close the meeting with prayer.

If you sense the members of the group would be uncomfortable praying out loud at this time, simply say a closing prayer yourself.

Make sure everybody knows the time and place for the next meeting. Remind them of the need for punctuality. (Did you end the meeting on time?) Serve refreshments (if it's not too late).

Follow Me ...
I'll Direct You

The purpose of this study is to help group members learn how to obey God in areas of life not directly addressed in the Bible.

This is the second study on the topic of obedience to God. This study deals with four principles that are helpful for making decisions in every area of life and every kind of decision. As you discuss "gray areas," avoid delving into the rightness or wrongness of specific issues (smoking, going to movies, and so on). Concentrate instead on the overriding principles to use in evaluating these activities. Group members will discover that even committed Christians may differ on what constitutes obedience to God. Every believer, however, shares the ambition to "make it our goal to please him" (2 Corinthians 5:9).

PRAYER

Open the meeting with prayer.

Bible

Have several volunteers share their observations and applications from 1 Peter 1.

Prayer

Invite each person to answer these questions:

What are five ways God has been faithful to you?

You may want to allow some time for everyone to write down his or her list of five ways before answering.

What are three qualities in your spouse or a close friend for which you are thankful?

Scripture Memory

See who can recite Luke 6:46.

PURPOSE

Lately your boss has been pressuring you to put in excessive overtime hours. You've been talking with him about Christ and feel a heightened responsibility to live rightly. You wonder: Should you submit to your boss's pressure to work at this hectic pace?

Your daughter, meanwhile, has been invited to the prom by a non-Christian guy. She is seventeen, and you want to give her the right amount of freedom without letting her make a poor decision. To what extent should you intervene as she decides whether to accept?

On the way home from work, you're reminded that your car is getting old and on the brink of falling apart. Sometime soon you will need to replace it. As a Christian, does it matter what kind of car you get or how much you spend on it?

Most of what we do in life is not regulated by specific commands of Scripture. We work, go to school, shop, and do many other activities that require us to use our judgment. How can we be sure of always making the right choices? What does it mean to obey Christ in the "gray" areas?

In this study, we will examine four steps we can use to help us obey God in any area of life.

Four Questions for Evaluating Our Actions

For more information on these four steps, see the book by LeRoy Eims, *Be The Leader You Were Meant To Be* (Wheaton, Ill.: Victor Books, 1975).

1   Is it beneficial in any way?

What are some examples of some activities that may be permissible but not necessarily beneficial? (1 Corinthians 6:12)

Watching television, certain social activities, and so on. Don't let the group argue about what should be on their list. Disagreements simply point out that these activities probably fall into the gray areas.

Note: Many activities clamor for our time. Most of them aren't specifically permitted or forbidden by God. A follower of Christ should evaluate such opportunities by asking whether they add anything to his or her life and/or relationship with God, and filter out activities that do not help.

What is something that is permissible to some but not beneficial for you?

Give everyone a chance to answer. Differences will help to illustrate the principle.

Can you think of a time recently that you participated in something that later you wish you hadn't because it wasn't profitable?

Share a personal example to get the discussion started.

2   Does it master me?

What are some activities that could master a person? (1 Corinthians 6:12)

Answers could include almost any activity, even good activities—reading, exercise, recreation. Everyone has areas of weakness they need to keep under control.

What activities do you need to guard against becoming master over you?

Encourage everyone to answer. Good activities can become addictive.

Note: God made all good things (Genesis 1:31), and gives us all things to enjoy (1 Timothy 6:17). But a follower of Christ should not let the enjoyment of good run his or her life. Hobbies, sports, food, sex, TV—just about any good activity can become an addiction. A good activity becomes destructive whenever it masters you.

3   Could it hurt someone else's walk with God?

Why should we limit our freedom? (1 Corinthians 10:24)

We must exercise our freedom in Christ responsibly.

How could a neutral or permissible activity hurt someone else? (1 Corinthians 8:13)

It could lure them into sin, cause them to violate their conscience, become addictive to them, or detract from their relationship with Christ.

Note: Cain asked, "Am I my brother's keeper?" (Genesis 4:9). For the Christian, the answer is yes. A follower of Christ should seek the good of others and avoid doing anything that causes another believer to sin.

4   Does it glorify God?

What does it mean to glorify God? (1 Corinthians 10:31)

To glorify God means to bring him honor. In many cases, this affects *how* we live more than exactly *what* we do. A follower of Christ should try to honor God in the midst of every activity.

How can everyday actions (like eating and drinking) bring glory to God?

Encourage group members to share incidents from their own life, either positive or negative.

BOTTOM LINE

**Following Jesus means evaluating the gray
areas of life according to Scripture.**

Bible

Read Matthew 16 three times.

Prayer

Day One: Adoration—Read Psalm 135 in an attitude of prayer.

Day Two: Confession—Identify a sin you struggle with regularly. Try to find a verse that speaks directly to that sin. Meditate on that verse.

Day Three: Thanksgiving—Thank God for who he made you—physically, relationally, mentally, and emotionally. Be specific in your prayer.

Scripture Memory

So whether you eat or drink or whatever you do, do it all for the glory of God.
1 Corinthians 10:31

PRAYER

Close the meeting in prayer.

3

Jesus, Lord of Who I Am

The purpose of this study is to help group members follow Jesus as supreme leader of their lives.

Salvation is described by the Scriptures as a free gift. Yet Jesus also spoke of discipleship as costly, and urged those who would follow him to count that cost. For Jesus, no final conflict existed between receiving his gracious forgiveness and following his exacting lordship. He knew he was offering to sinful people something they couldn't earn themselves—yet as their Lord he was calling them to a life of service that required obedience at every turn. The concept of receiving the gift without deference to the giver was unthinkable. To take part in the relationship (Savior and Forgiver) without embracing *all* he is (including Master and Leader) would be as ridiculous as going through a marriage ceremony without anticipating a lifetime of loving and serving your spouse. Technically, you don't become a Christian by living a good life. But would it make any sense to become married with no intention of responding to your spouse? Does it make sense to receive Christ without responding daily in obedience to his commands?

PRAYER

Open the meeting with prayer, or have a volunteer do so.

Bible

Have group members share their observations and applications from Matthew 16.

Prayer

Adoration: Ask group members what it meant for them to read Psalm 135 in an attitude of prayer.

Confession: Ask whether group members were able to find verses that speak to specific areas of temptation for them.

Thanksgiving: Ask, **For what did you thank God?**

If time permits, ask group members what they are enjoying most about the prayer portion of their appointments with God. Then ask what difficulties (such as scheduling, mind wandering, etc.) they are having. Spend some time talking about how to meet the challenges that keep them from praying regularly.

Scripture Memory

Have everyone recite 1 Corinthians 10:31.

PURPOSE

In the hearts of countless Americans, few events are more fascinating than a romance between celebrities. The press eagerly snatches up every details of the courtship and reports them to a fascinated public. The couple makes orchestrated public appearances, exuding radiant smiles and tender looks for one another as the photographers take picture after picture. Finally they announce wedding plans, vowing that their relationship will last forever. The ceremony is a lavish spectacle, attended by admiring peers and surrounded by fans who hope to catch a glimpse of their idols. Yes, this must be love . . . or is it?

Soon, disturbing stories of discord between the couple emerge. They are seen less frequently together, and soon it becomes evident that the fairy-tale romance has lost its magic. Rumors circulate that both partners are seeing other people. Within a year, the stories are borne out by an announcement of a pending divorce. Recriminations fly between the couple in the press, and reporters find fresh copy digging up the details about new relationships that each partner has begun. Why do so many romances among the famous (and not-so-famous) end in disaster?

One obvious answer might be that people fail to perceive the commitment necessary to maintain a relationship. It is easy to make that first step, to pledge lifelong devotion to another person. Yet when problems and conflicts happen, it requires self-sacrifice and hard work to make those commitments stick. Our Christian lives also require that kind of devotion if we are to remain effective servants for God. In this study, you will gain an understanding of what it means to be a disciple of the *Lord* Jesus Christ, submitted to his lordship.

STUDY

The key verse for this study is Matthew 16:24—*"Then Jesus said to his disciples, 'If anyone would come after me, he must deny himself and take up his cross and follow me.'"*

If you were with the disciples when Jesus said this, how might you have reacted?

Deny Self

What does it mean to deny self?

> To deny is to say no to something. To deny oneself means to deny one's selfish nature.

What should we deny or say no to?

> Self-gratification.

> Note: God wants us to say no to our sinful desires. We're commanded to say no to selfish tendencies (the part of us that wants to sin) as much as we are to harmful activities. Our natural desires pull us toward sin. Jesus says that to follow him is to keep a tight rein on those desires.

In what area has it been hard for you to deny yourself lately?

Encourage discussion by volunteering a personal example if appropriate.

Note: There is a difference between self-gratification and self-care. Self-care is essential to one's well being and is a God-glorifying response to the gift of life. Self-indulgence is destructive to our well being as it is born out our sinful nature.

Take Up Your Cross

What did it mean for a person to literally take up a cross in Jesus' day?

In Jesus' day, a criminal sentenced to die by crucifixion was made to carry the wooden crossbeam to the execution site. Thus, to Jesus' audience, "take up his cross" literally meant to begin a painful and certain journey toward death.

What truth about walking with God was Jesus trying to communicate when he said take up your cross?

A Christian must be a living sacrifice for God (Luke 9:24). We should be surrendered to the sometimes difficult reality that his agenda is more important than our own.

Why is it uncomfortable or unnatural for each of us to take up our cross?

You have to die to yourself. Our nature and our culture tells us that we should not let ourselves be uncomfortable.

Why is it important to take up your cross daily?

Our struggle with sin never ends. Yesterday's victories don't guarantee success today.

How does taking up your cross relate to family life?

We should fulfill our God-given responsibilities as a spouse and parent, enduring with grace all the costs those responsibilities entail.

Follow Christ

What are some other words that mean the same as "follow"?

Imitate, mimic, pursue, reflect, walk closely with, chase after, conform to, comply with. To follow Jesus is to "follow the leader"—to do what he does.

In what ways do you find it easy to imitate Jesus?

Take time to get an answer from everyone.

Note: Jesus always did what the Father wanted him to do. One aspect of following Jesus is to imitate his obedience to the Father.

In what ways is it difficult to imitate Jesus?

Encourage specific responses.

In what area of life do you want to become more like Jesus? How?

Invite group members to help each other on this point.

BOTTOM LINE

**Following Jesus means denying sin and dying
to its pleasure in order to glorify God.**

YOUR WALK WITH GOD

Bible

Study Matthew 19, especially 19:16-26, "The Rich Young Man."

Prayer

Day One: Adoration—Paraphrase Psalm 139:1-6 as a prayer of adoration to God. Come up with a title for this part of the psalm.

Day Two: Confession—On three separate occasions during the week, look back over the previous day's events and conversations to identify anything you need to confess.

Day Three: Thanksgiving—Thank God for what God has done for you.

Scripture Memory

Then Jesus said to his disciples, "If anyone would come after me, he must deny himself and take up his cross and follow me."   Matthew 16:24

In the next study we will take a look at what it means for Jesus as lord of what we have. To prepare, think about the possessions you would most hate to lose.

PRAYER

Close the meeting in prayer.

4

Jesus, Lord of What I Have

The purpose of this study is to help group members see Jesus as ultimate owner of all they possess.

Your group members could potentially span the spectrum of wealth, from relatively poor to relatively rich. The amount of money we possess is not the issue, but whether what we have is placed under the lordship of Christ. Some may be like the rich young ruler—captivated by and used to all the money they have. Others may be captivated by all the money they *don't* have. The bottom line is that Jesus is owner and sovereign over all we have. A mature follower of Christ uses his or her material resources for the benefit of the kingdom of God.

PRAYER

Open the meeting with prayer.

Bible

Invite volunteers to share their observations and applications from Matthew 19.

Prayer

Adoration: Ask your group members, **What titles did you give to Psalm 139:1-6?**

Invite group members to share their paraphrases of Psalm 139:1-6.

Confession: Ask your group members, **Was it helpful or unhelpful to reflect back on the week and recall sins that should be confessed?**

Thanksgiving: Ask your group members, **What did you thank God for this week?**

Scripture Memory

Review Matthew 16:24 with your group.

PURPOSE

To those who knew him, the rich young man had no money problem. He had power, comfort, and prestige. Every material need he had was easily met. Yet something inside him sensed that he still needed something else to be truly satisfied. He came to Jesus hoping for affirmation and comfort. But when Jesus exposed the source of his restlessness, the ruler balked. He probably could have made any other sacrifice, but being required to surrender his wealth was too threatening, for it was the foundation of his security. His money problem was not a lack of means, but rather an excessive dependence on it.

Christians sometimes have the same struggles as the rich young man. Reliance on wealth can create bondage and anxiety for believers as well as for nonbelievers. But a big part of being Christ's disciple is handling your resources in a way that honors God. That's a tough challenge. In this study you will learn a way to meet that challenge.

Begin by reading Matthew 19:16-26 as a group. Then discuss the following questions.

Rich Young Man

What various details do we know about the man who came to see Jesus? (Matthew 19:16-26)

- He was young.
- He was wealthy.
- He was religious.
- He wanted eternal life.
- He was aware of the fact that he was missing something.
- He was respectful of Jesus (called him "Teacher").

What did Jesus accomplish by his response to the young man's question? (Matthew 19:17)

Jesus wanted him to focus on the right standard—God. The young man was looking for a "good work" to do. Jesus made it clear that only God is capable of truly good works—ours are tainted by sin. By looking at God instead of works, he would begin to see what true goodness really is. And it would deliver him of his self-righteous assumption that he had that goodness within himself apart from repentance and forgiveness.

Why do you think Jesus listed the commandments he did? (Matthew 19:18-19)

Jesus had spoken earlier about goodness in general, and now about relationships. He was "narrowing the field," so to speak, setting the man up for a challenge regarding the one main commandment he had flagrantly violated.

Why did the man insist that he still lacked something? (Matthew 19:20-21)

He obviously *felt* it. He wanted to be perfect, completely acceptable to God, and knew something was missing even though he could claim obedience to the laws of Moses.

According to Jesus, what was the man's problem? (Matthew 19:21)

The man needed to keep the first commandment, "You shall have no other gods before me" (Exodus 20:3). In this sense, he was guilty of idolatry. Imagine another man coming to Jesus exactly like the rich young ruler—except that he is willing to do what Jesus asked. Suppose the man responded to Jesus' command by saying, "I'll do it, Lord—I'll do whatever you say." If he had said that and done what Jesus asked, he would have shown that he had no other gods in his life.

Why did Jesus say that it is hard for rich people to enter the kingdom of heaven? (Matthew 19:23-24)

It is human nature to allow ourselves to be mastered by money. Once we have it, it has us, and we don't naturally want to let go of it.

Why were the disciples so incredulous at Jesus' comments? (Matthew 19:25-26)

The disciples had assumed that wealth signaled God's blessing. If people who received God's blessing couldn't be saved, then how could anyone? In effect he was saying, "Don't think rich people are more favored by God; as a matter of fact, they will have a harder time resisting the temptation of idolatry. But God's grace can save anyone."

What do you most want to remember about Jesus' talk with the rich young man?

Invite everyone to answer. Each person may be impressed by different aspects of the story. One central principle is that we should submit all our material resources to Christ.

BOTTOM LINE

Following Jesus means he is master over all we have.

YOUR WALK WITH GOD

Bible

Read Matthew 20 three times, noting observations and applications.

Prayer

Day One: Adoration—Paraphrase Psalm 139:7-12 and pray through it. Come up with a title for this part of the psalm.

Day Two: Supplication—List two or three sins you would especially like to defeat in your life. Ask God to replace these with characteristics of his.

Day Three: Thanksgiving—Thank God for one thing or person you've taken for granted lately.

Scripture Memory

Review the memory verses you have learned so far in *"Follow Me!"*: Luke 6:46; 1 Corinthians 10:31; and Matthew 16:24.

In the next study we will take a look at some of the benefits of following Jesus. What do you value most about your relationship with God? What "nice extras" have you experienced that you did not expect when you first became a Christian?

PRAYER

Close the meeting in prayer.

ON YOUR OWN

A Word About Finances

The Bible has more to say about money than just about any other single subject. Maybe that's because it holds the potential for great kingdom gain—or great personal loss. Marriages break up over it, careers are shaped by it, needs are supplied through it, and lives are shipwrecked mismanaging it.

An integral part of being a disciple of Jesus Christ is handling your resources in a God-honoring way. In our culture, that poses a tough challenge. Some of you may be like the rich young man in tonight's study and do not yet recognize your obeisance and obedience to another god. Or you may tend to the opposite extreme: always longing but never having. You may worship the same god as the rich young man, only you do so from a distance. Many will be somewhere in the middle. Whatever your situation, it is important to note: *Proper money management—stewardship—is essential for a mature follower of Jesus Christ.*

Jesus, Lord of All

The purpose of this study is to help group members appreciate the benefits of following Christ.

The previous two studies highlighted the costs of following Jesus. This one balances that expense with the benefits.

Some of your group members may be uncomfortable discussing "benefits" of following Christ. This may be because they don't want to compare the decision to follow Christ to a decision to purchase something. After all, the Christian life is one of sacrifice. Why cheapen it with talk of benefits?

But the benefits are real, and believers should be aware of them. It's important to accept the blessings that God offers to us and thank him for them.

PRAYER

Have several group members open the meeting with prayer.

Bible

Ask: **What observations and applications did you make from Matthew 20?**

Prayer

Adoration: Have each person who is willing read his or her paraphrase of Psalm 139:7-12.

Supplication: Have each person share a character prayer request, and then pray for one another.

Thanksgiving: Have everyone say what thing or person they had taken for granted and thanked God.

Scripture Memory

Have everyone recite Luke 6:46; 1 Corinthians 10:31; and Matthew 16:24.

PURPOSE

Have you ever signed up for a "free offer" only to find out you were going to be billed $19.95 for it? Perhaps you were one of the lucky winners of a "free gift" only to find out you had to listen to a two hour sales pitch to claim it. "There's no such thing as a free lunch," as the saying goes. You pay a price for almost everything. This is as true of following Christ as it is in any other area of life.

The last two studies went into detail about the costs of being a disciple of Christ. Those costs are: (1) deny yourself, (2) take up your cross, (3) follow Christ, (4) submit all you have to the Lord. It is not hard to see from that list that the cost is substantial.

But the cost is also worth paying. Jesus didn't hold back from telling his disciples of the benefits of following him. In this study you'll learn about those benefits.

Review the last two studies and prepare the group for this week's study by discussing the following two questions about the costs of following Christ.

What are the costs of following Christ?

Answers include: denying self, taking up one's cross, imitating Christ, and yielding what you have to the Lord.

What did you have to give up to become a Christian?

Invite everyone to contribute an answer.

We need to keep perspective on what the "cost" of following Jesus really amounts to. It can be compared to the cost of going to the hospital and having a life-threatening tumor removed. Of course there are costs involved—but consider what the alternative would cost you!

Benefits of Following Christ

1   God's Provision

What benefit did Jesus promise to all who seek his kingdom first? (Matthew 6:33)

We have the promise that God will meet our needs.

2   Freedom

What benefit is there in believing the truth about Christ? (John 8:32)

We are set free. Sin isn't just some bad act we do—it's a power that enslaves us. Through submission to Jesus Christ, we are liberated—set free from sin's power.

3   Peace of Mind

In what kinds of circumstances does Jesus promise us peace of mind? (John 14:27)

Jesus' peace is not the absence of conflict or problems, but the presence of Christ in the middle of them. The hope and assurance of a bright future with Jesus gives us peace of mind.

4 Joy

What is unique about Jesus' joy? (John 15:11)

The joy Christ gives transcends life's ups and downs: it enables us to be content because it is rooted in God's sovereignty.

5 Peace with God

What is peace with God? (Romans 5:1-2)

Every Christian has a permanent, eternal, unbreakable relationship with God. It is not dependent on *our* works, but upon Christ's finished work. Our sins are forgiven and we are justified by grace.

6 God's Love

How did God show his love for us? (Romans 5:5-8)

Christ died for us when we were still sinners. By loving us under such conditions, we need never doubt that God cares for us just as we are.

7 Hope of Heaven

What does the future hold for those without the hope of heaven? (Romans 5:9-10)

Salvation from sin and hell. Through Jesus' death, we are saved from God's wrath. None of us could stand on our own merit before God's standard of perfection; we would have no chance of entering heaven, and would incur God's wrath. But through Christ, we are saved from condemnation.

8 Character Development

How does God change our character? (Romans 8:28-29)

God uses our experiences to hone and remake us into someone stronger and more usable. Even hard times can have a higher purpose when we walk with him during those trials.

9 Access to God

What assurance do we have about our prayers? (Hebrews 4:16)

God will hear and respond.

Note: When Jesus died, the veil of the temple in Jerusalem tore in two, showing that the barrier between us and God had been removed. Through Christ, we have direct access to God. We can speak to him at any time, in any place, about anything—and know we will be heard.

Conclusion

Why is it worth paying the costs of following Christ? (1 Corinthians 9:24-27)

> The rewards are permanent, unlike the rewards we get from the world, which are temporary.

If you had to single out only one, which of these benefits would you select as the most meaningful to you?

> Allow time for all to answer.

BOTTOM LINE

Following Jesus means we know: "He is no fool who gives up what he cannot keep to gain what he cannot lose." –Jim Elliot

---

YOUR WALK WITH GOD

Bible

Read and study Matthew 21 three times. As you read, let these two questions guide your observations and applications: (1) In what way were these events the "beginning of the end" for Jesus? (2) What do you learn about Jesus from this chapter?

Prayer

Day One: Adoration—Paraphrase Psalm 139:13-18 and pray through it.

Day Two: Confession—On three separate occasions, focus on the previous day's events and let the Holy Spirit convict you of whatever sins need cleansing.

Day Three: Thanksgiving—In your prayer, complete the sentence, "Heavenly Father, thank you for the opportunities I have to _____."

Scripture Memory

Everyone who competes in the games goes into strict training. They do it to get a crown that will not last; but we do it to get a crown that will last forever.   1 Corinthians 9:25

In the next study we will take a closer look at the expectations we have for God. Do you expect him to give you a life free from difficulty? Do you sometimes find yourself thinking that God owes you something? What do you expect God to do for you?

PRAYER

Close the meeting in prayer.

The Beginning of the End

OVERVIEW

The purpose of this study is to help group members understand the importance of Palm Sunday and its significance for us today.

This study will examine the expectation of the crowds in Jesus day that he would liberate them from Rome. Jesus accomplished his mission on earth, but many were not satisfied with what he did because their expectations were not met. People still have unmet expectations for Jesus today. What do they demand from God today? What makes them upset or angry at God? This may lead to deeper discussion later.

PRAYER

Open the meeting with prayer.

REVIEW

Bible

Discuss your group's answers to the questions on Matthew 21.

1. In what way were these events the "beginning of the end" for Jesus?

2. What do you learn about Jesus from this chapter?

Note: You may want to save these questions for the discussion itself.

Prayer

Adoration: Have several people read their paraphrase of Psalm 139:13-18.

Confession: Ask the group, **What are you learning from spending regular time confessing your sins?**

Thanksgiving: Ask the group, **For what opportunities did you thank God?**

Scripture Memory

Have the group recite 1 Corinthians 9:25.

PURPOSE

Expectations have a way of setting us up for disappointment. Consider, for example, some of the actions you expect from your family or friends—perhaps keeping you informed of their whereabouts, or taking out the trash every Thursday night. Whether these expectations are realistic doesn't matter; you have come to depend on them. What happens when they aren't met?

Palm Sunday was a clash of expectations. Jesus had arrived in Jerusalem six days before the Passover, one of the most important holidays in the Jewish calendar. Thousands of people had crammed into Jerusalem to observe the feast. Shortly before he entered the city, he had raised Lazarus from the dead; when people heard about it, anticipation built for what he would do next. Many people fully expected him to liberate them from Rome. He was greeted by a throng of admiring locals.

But those expectations did not match Jesus' mission. Rather than coming to conquer Rome, he had come to conquer sin; his aims were spiritual, not political. Some sort of letdown was inevitable. And so, when it became clear that Jesus would not use his power for nationalistic ends, popularity swung to the religious leaders. Festive Palm Sunday was, ironically, the beginning of the end for Jesus.

In this study, we will focus on the events of Palm Sunday, one of the key events in God's unfolding plan of salvation.

The Triumphal Entry

How did the crowds greet Jesus as he was riding into the city of Jerusalem? (Matthew 21:1-11)

> They gave him a king's reception, saying, "Hosanna to the Son of David!" as he rode by.

Why did the crowds gather to greet Jesus? (John 12:9-11, 17-18)

> They had heard of the raising of Lazarus—something which concerned the Pharisees and excited most others. Hearing of Jesus' power made many people hope that Jesus would free them from Rome, for if he had the power to raise someone from the dead, maybe he would use that power to conquer their enemies. They were honoring Jesus for what he'd already done in bringing Lazarus back to life, hoping he'd go the next step and seize political power also.

What is the significance of Jesus riding in on a donkey? (Zechariah 9:9)

> The prophet Zechariah predicted this very act by the Messiah. A horse was the customary mount for a conquering ruler; a donkey colt was a symbol of humility. Because "Messiah" still had a "conquering hero" concept attached to it, this was one more way for Jesus to reiterate his peaceful, nonpolitical agenda for his mission as king of God's people. He was not there to stir up revolt, but to conquer hearts, minds, and souls with sacrificial love.

Why did the crowds say what they did about Jesus? (Matthew 21:9-11)

> "Son of David" was a title for the Messiah who would rule over the reborn nation of Israel. "Hosanna" was a shout of praise meaning *Save us, O Lord!* They believed he came "in the name of the Lord" (see Psalm 118:25). All of this says that they recognized his uniqueness, though it is hard to tell to what extent they understood the mission of their Messiah.

The Beginning of the End

Now skip ahead to Matthew 27:15-26, the story of Jesus' public trial and condemnation. Read or summarize this event and then discuss the following questions.

Nearly a week later, after Jesus had been arrested and tried, the crowd condemned Jesus to die (Matthew 27:15-26). How could Jesus be rejected by the crowd so soon after he was hailed as their king?

There are several reasons for Jesus' rejection on Good Friday:

- The religious leaders had incited the crowd to ask for Barabbas's release (Matthew 27:20).

- The crowd that condemned Jesus may not have been the same as the one that cheered him a week earlier.

- Jesus had not fulfilled the popular expectations people had at that time for their Messiah.

We sometimes want God to act in ways that compromise his character. What are some examples of expecting what we shouldn't from God?

Encourage group members to share their answers. Some examples include expecting God to:

- give us all our desires

- make all our troubles go away

- overlook sin

- deliver us from all consequences of our sin

- answer all prayer when we want and in the way we want.

- keep us from experiencing loss or pain.

When has there been a time when you expected God to act a certain way and he refused?

Lead off with an example of your own, and then invite group members to share.

In what ways do you need to adjust your expectations of God at this point in your life?

Invite all group members to share.

Note: You should emphasize at this point that God is not a means to our ends, but rather we are a means to his. It is when we allow ourselves to be used for his purposes that our lives will take on meaning and a sense of accomplishment. In this way God is glorified and we are fulfilled.

How should we adjust our expectations in order to serve God totally? (John 12:24-26)

> We need more than an adjustment of expectations—we need to reorder them so that we seek to serve God above all else. Jesus tells us that to serve him we must follow him (John 12:26).

In what ways are you a means to God's ends today?

> Encourage everyone to respond.

When has God used a painful event in your life to accomplish his purposes in or through you?

> Start the discussion with a personal example.

BOTTOM LINE

Following Jesus means we must fulfill God's expectations.

YOUR WALK WITH GOD

Bible

Read Matthew 22–23 three times, noting observations and applications.

Prayer

Day One: Adoration—Paraphrase Psalm 139:19-24 as a prayer of adoration.

Day Two: Supplication—Pray for sensitivity to God's purposes in your life.

Day Three: Thanksgiving—List the purposes God has for your life—all the ones you can think of. Thank him for his care.

Scripture Memory

For whoever wants to save his life will lose it, but whoever loses his life for me will find it.   Matthew 16:25

In the next study we will take a look at the opposition that Jesus experienced during his ministry. When has your following Christ produced negative reactions in others? How did you respond? What problems or opportunities did this create for you?

PRAYER

Close the meeting in prayer.

Jesus Under Attack

OVERVIEW

The purpose of this study is to help group members learn why people oppose Jesus, and how we as believers should respond.

Most Christians experience some kind of opposition to their faith, just as Jesus did. Be aware that group members who identify publicly with Jesus will probably understand this study more readily than those who, for whatever reason, keep a lower profile.

PRAYER

Open the meeting with prayer.

REVIEW

Bible

Invite group members to share observations and applications from Matthew 22–23.

Prayer

Adoration: Have each person share his or her paraphrase of Psalm 139:19-24, along with any observations about how this enabled him or her to worship.

Supplication: Ask group members what purposes of God they have become more sensitive to.

Thanksgiving: Ask the group, **For which of God's purposes did you thank him this week?**

Scripture Memory

Have everyone recite Matthew 16:25.

PURPOSE

Most people want to be liked by somebody—to feel affirmed, appreciated, important. Who hasn't done something with the hope that "so-and-so will really be pleased"? Whether it be your parents, your boss, the crowd, or a personal mentor, the desire to please can be a great motivator.

But being liked was not at the top of Jesus' priorities. Rather, he did what was right—what the Father wanted him to do—at all costs, and taught others that they should do the same. His healings did gain him many admirers, but he did not heal them to win their favor or to seek their recognition. While the crowds liked him, his hard stand against hypocrisy exposed the religious leaders of his day, and over time Jesus gained more and more enemies. While Jesus knew this, he never altered his deeds or words to halt the defection.

Christians who live their faith openly will encounter opposition too. Those trapped in darkness hate the light. Just as the world rejected Jesus, it will reject those who follow him. Because rejection from the world is inevitable, we should do all we can to prepare for it.

In this study, you will learn how to handle opposition by seeing the way Jesus was opposed and how he responded.

Jesus under Attack

How did the religious leaders try to trap Jesus? (Matthew 21:23-27; 22:15-46)

The Pharisees, Sadducees, and Herodians publicly challenged Jesus' authority and used trick questions to try to embarrass him. Specifically,

> The Pharisees and Herodians sent their followers to ask Jesus trick questions (22:16-17).

> The Sadducees asked a trick question about marriage at the resurrection (22:23-28).

> The Pharisees tried to get Jesus to stumble on the question of which was the greatest commandment (22:34-36).

Why did the Pharisees and others try to trap Jesus? (Matthew 22:15-46)

Jesus posed a major threat to their power and influence.

Note: The *Pharisees* were popular religious leaders and teachers. They tried to make the Law of Moses apply directly to their day by making up a large number of additional rules and regulations to govern every possible circumstance. Unfortunately, they had become arrogant and more concerned with keeping their rules than with keeping the commandments God had given them. Jesus' message undermined the pretensions of the Pharisees. Because they had a great deal of power and influence over the people of Israel, these religious leaders wanted to discredit Jesus and eventually put him to death because they felt threatened by his popular appeal and radical message.

The *Sadducees* were a group of wealthy, ruling-class religious leaders who believed only in the five books of Moses (Genesis, Exodus, Leviticus, Numbers, Deuteronomy). They did not believe in the afterlife or in a future resurrection. Their concerns about Jesus were similar to those of the Herodians—they did not want to upset the political status quo.

The *Herodians* were Jewish people loyal to Herod, the local Roman ruler. They opposed Jesus because they feared he would stir up the crowds against Herod.

In short, all three groups wanted Jesus trapped so they could maintain their position and power.

Jesus' Response

For what did Jesus condemn the religious leaders? (Matthew 23:1-39)

- They were hypocrites (23:3).

- They required impossible deeds of people (23:4).

- They did their good deeds for show (23:5-7).

- They craved recognition (23:6-7).

- By their hypocrisy and misguided application of the Law, they blocked many others from coming to God (23:13).

- Their hairsplitting system of oaths disguised their real values—greater love for money than for God (23:16-22).

- They emphasized minor details of spiritual practice and totally missed real obedience (23:23-24).

- They mistook ceremonial cleanliness for true goodness (23:25-26).

- They were outwardly good, but inwardly corrupt (23:27-28).

- They didn't see that their own opposition to Jesus was worse than their ancestors' opposition to the prophets (23:29-31).

What can we learn from the Pharisees' negative example?

Discuss everyone's answers.

Conclusion

What sort of opposition does Jesus receive today?

- People disbelieve in him.

- People characterize Christians as odd (though the reputation is sometimes deserved!).

- People oppose what Christians stand for.

What can you learn from the way Jesus responded to opposition?

- Doing God's will is not always popular.

- Following Jesus will draw fire from people who feel threatened by you.

- Doing God's will is worth the price of making some people uncomfortable.

Can you think of a time in the past when you experienced opposition for being a Christian?

Give a personal example.

Why might experiencing opposition be a sign of obedience to God? (2 Timothy 3:12)

Paul told us that anyone who attempts to live a godly life for Jesus Christ will be persecuted. There seems to be no exception to this rule!

In what ways can Christians bring unnecessary criticism and opposition upon themselves?

Being disrespectful of people, intolerant of other values, trying to force your faith on others, and so on.

BOTTOM LINE

Following Jesus means you can expect the world to oppose you.

YOUR WALK WITH GOD

Bible

Read and study Matthew 24–25 three times.

Prayer

This week, it's your turn to come up with creative prayer ideas! Use the basic A.C.T.S. format, but identify your own specific emphases. Be prepared to share what you did for each next week.

Adoration: _____

Confession: _____

Thanksgiving: _____

Supplication: _____

Scripture Memory

Blessed are you when men hate you, when they exclude you and insult you and reject your name as evil, because of the Son of Man.   Luke 6:22

In the next study we will learn about Christ's promise to return. What emotions does that event evoke in you?

PRAYER

You or a group member close the meeting with prayer.

Ready For His Return

OVERVIEW

The purpose of this study is to help group members be ready for Christ's return.

It's easy to get caught up in speculation over the timing of Christ's return. Do your best to avoid it in your meeting. Jesus did not teach about his return to tease us into figuring out when it would happen, but to inspire us to be faithful while waiting, no matter how long the wait may be.

PRAYER

Open the meeting with prayer.

REVIEW

Bible

Have group members tell what sort of observations and applications they made from Matthew 24–25.

Prayer

Ask each group member to pick one idea for prayer that he or she came up with and share it with the group. Then briefly pray as a group for one another's persistence in prayer.

Scripture Memory

Have everyone recite Luke 6:22.

PURPOSE

We are always getting ready for something. We get ready for bed, for work, for dinner, for retirement. We prepare meals and prepare for dinner guests. The more important the upcoming event, the more time and energy we spend preparing.

Jesus has not finished what he set out to do among us. When Jesus ascended into heaven, he didn't leave this earth permanently. When all other great religious leaders died, they left behind their teachings, their example, their followers, and their corpses. Only Jesus rose—bodily—from the dead. And only Jesus will return—bodily—to earth.

When Jesus does return, he will terminate history as we know it. He will answer all our questions. He will assume his final place as Lord as every knee bows. He will expose and judge all evil deeds. And he will fulfill all of God's promises.

Following Jesus means living in the light of that truth. Not only is our Savior alive, and not only is he with us through the Holy Spirit—he is also coming again!

STUDY

Be on the Alert for His Coming

What do you observe about the second coming of Christ from Matthew 24:26-35?

It will be preceded by many traumatic events.

Note: Jesus described many of these events in detail. Note your group members' observations about this passage, but don't spend a lot of time analyzing the details. The important point here is to observe that there will be an increase in certain signs before Jesus returns.

In what ways can you ready yourself for Christ's coming?

This question is worth spending some time on. Following are some possible answers:

- Loosen your grip on material things. Do not let possessions distract you from eternal things—easily forgotten in the chase after "goodies."

- Stay close to Christ. Be ready to face him right now.

- Invest for eternal rewards. Only God, his Word, angels, and people will last forever. Heaven and earth and all its stuff will pass away.

- Spread the news about Christ. Make your life a representation of Christ to others. Offer the invitation to an eternity in heaven to as many as will hear.

- Prepare for hard times. Strengthen your own faith every day.

How can you remind yourself that Jesus will return?

Request specific answers and see what people say.

What distracts you from being "on the alert"?

Remind group members that it is easy to get caught up in the here and now unless we take pains to remember eternity.

The Two Kinds of Slaves

What do the main characters in this parable represent? (Matthew 24:45-51)

Faithful slave: hard-working Christian who is serving the Lord when Jesus returns.

Evil slave: someone who takes Jesus' absence as a license to indulge in an evil life-style.

Master: the Lord himself.

In what ways have you been like each of these slaves?

Allow sufficient time for discussion.

Note: Jesus told this parable because he knew he would not come back immediately, and he wanted to help his followers not lose heart in the interim. He wanted to assure those who are faithful to him that they will be rewarded, while those who squander his absence will be justly judged.

The Ten Virgins

Who are the main characters in this parable? (Matthew 25:1-13)

> Bridegroom: Jesus.
>
> Five wise virgins: Christians who plan for the long haul.
>
> Five foolish virgins: those unprepared for Judgment Day.

How does this parable challenge you?

> The main point is that we should take Jesus' return seriously and be ready for it at all times.
>
> Note: The lamps do not really represent anything other than preparedness for Christ's return—that is, long-term faithfulness to him rather than just a short-term enthusiasm. Jesus wants people to be ready when he returns, even though there is a delay in his second coming.

The Talents

Who are the main characters in the Parable of the Talents? (Matthew 25:14-30)

> Master on a journey: the Lord.
>
> Slave with five talents: someone with great capacity.
>
> Slave with two talents: someone with less capacity.
>
> Slave with one talent: someone with minimal capacity.

Where do you need to be more faithful with what God has given to you?

> Encourage everyone to respond with specific answers.
>
> Note: God has given *everyone* something to invest for him. The wicked person figures God will take back his life at the end anyway and doesn't do anything. But a true believer wants to be fruitful using whatever resources he or she has to further God's kingdom. The lazy slave's downfall was his *laziness*—he was out to avoid any obligation to serve God, and covered up his inaction with excuses.

Conclusion

What simple step or activity could you do this week that would help you be more prepared for Christ's coming?

> Invite everyone to contribute an answer.

YOUR WALK WITH GOD

Bible

Read and study Matthew 26 three times.

Prayer

Day One: Adoration—During the events described in Matthew 26, right before he died on the cross, Jesus said no to many natural human desires. What were those desires? What other godly attributes did he display in resisting those temptations?

Day Two: Confession—To what selfish desires do you need to die in order to live for God?

Day Three: Supplication—Pray for God to help you die to the desires you listed.

Scripture Memory

Review the following memory verses: 1 Corinthians 9:25; Matthew 16:25; and Luke 6:22.

Next study is about Jesus being betrayed and his commitment to doing the Father's will. What about God's will do you struggle with? What does it mean to pray "your will be done"?

PRAYER

Close the meeting with prayer.

Betrayed!

OVERVIEW

The purpose of this study is to help group members understand the final hours before Jesus' crucifixion and, like him, commit themselves to doing God's will.

There is probably no higher drama in the Bible than the story of Jesus' betrayal. And there is probably no lower moment in history than that night. This study takes you and your group through the final preparations by Judas and the chief priests to arrest Jesus, and climaxes at the point in Jesus' trial where Peter denied him. It is a very dismal chapter, but one full of important truths—and warnings.

PRAYER

Open the meeting with prayer.

REVIEW

Bible

Have group members briefly share their observations and applications from Matthew 26.

Prayer

Adoration: Ask group members, **What human desires did Jesus say no to in his final hours on earth?** Note as many answers as you can. Here are some possibilities:

- Desire for honor and recognition
- Desire for pity
- Desire to have one's own way
- Desire for power
- Desire to be proven right

Confession: Ask group members, **What selfish desires did you identify as getting in the way of living for God?**

Supplication: Take a few moments now to pray for one another, asking God for help in resisting our sinful desires.

Scripture Memory

Have someone recite each of the following passages: 1 Corinthians 9:25; Matthew 16:25; and Luke 6:22.

PURPOSE

Life is hard. Beside its joys and rewards come difficulties and disappointments. And getting older often means taking on more of life's burdens, not fewer of them. "What a heavy burden God has laid on men!" (Ecclesiastes 1:13).

Jesus' life was no different. In fact, his very mission was to suffer and die—unjustly. The price he paid—separation from God—cost him more than we can imagine. His suffering was intense not just while he was on the cross, but even before, as in the Garden of Gethsemane he faced the certainty of the pain he would suffer.

Yet Jesus willingly went through with his mission. Why? Because he wanted to do his Father's will more than anything else. His agonizing prayer, "Not as I will, but as you will" (Matthew 26:39), was not just a prayer. It was his life and mission.

This study takes you through the final preparations by Judas and the chief priests to arrest Jesus, and climaxes at the point in Jesus' trial where Peter denies him. It is a dismal chapter—but as such, it is full of important warnings. No can ever safely consider himself or herself bulletproof against the attacks of Satan. Rather, our prayer must perpetually be, "not as I will, but as you will."

STUDY

Jesus' Final Hours

Matthew 26 describes eight separate incidents in Jesus' final hours of life on earth. They are:

1. The plot to kill Jesus (Matthew 26:1-5)
2. The costly perfume controversy (Matthew 26:6-13)
3. Judas arranges to betray Jesus (Matthew 26:14-16)
4. The Last Supper (Matthew 26:17-30)
5. The Garden of Gethsemane (Matthew 26:31-46)
6. The betrayal and arrest of Jesus (Matthew 26:47-56)
7. Jesus' trial before Caiaphas (Matthew 26:57-68)
8. Peter's denial (Matthew 26:69-75)

1 The plot to kill Jesus

Why did the Jewish religious leaders plot to kill Jesus? (Matthew 26:1-5)

> They said they were trying him for blasphemy (for claiming to be the Son of God), but in reality they wanted to stop him from discrediting them. Jesus' teaching exposed their hypocrisy and challenged their authority. They would not tolerate that.

> Note that they wanted to wait until after the crowds had left so Jesus' popularity would not thwart their plan (26:5).

In what way is Jesus' lordship a threat to our authority over ourselves?

> Jesus wants to rule our lives. We want to rule our lives. Eventually, the two will clash and one must win.

2   The costly perfume controversy

Why did Jesus defend the woman for pouring expensive perfume on him? (Matthew 26:6-13)

- Her deed showed devotion and worship.

- Her deed acknowledged the fact that Jesus would soon die—a fact his disciples had yet to accept.

Why is it important to be open to what God wants instead of our own view of what is practical or good?

Sometimes love is very impractical—but love is God's highest value, not practicality!

3   Judas arranges to betray Jesus

How did Jesus' opponents get their opportunity to arrest Jesus? (Matthew 26:14-16)

Judas struck a deal with them so that they could arrest Jesus without risking the interference of a crowd.

4   The Last Supper

What was the significance of Jesus' Last Supper with the disciples? (Matthew 26:17-30; John 13:1-17)

- Judas left to betray Jesus.

- Jesus created a memory of affection and unity with his friends.

- Jesus demonstrated love and servanthood.

- Jesus established a sacrament.

Why should we remember Jesus' Last Supper?

- It is Jesus' desire.

- It reminds us of Jesus' obedience to the point of death.

- It reminds us of all Jesus did for us, especially his sacrifice.

- It reminds us to serve one another.

5   The Garden of Gethsemane

What do you notice about Jesus and his disciples in the garden of Gethsemane? (Matthew 26:31-46)

- Prophecy was being fulfilled.

- The disciples made commitments they didn't keep.

- Jesus wanted Peter, James, and John—his inner circle—to be with him in prayer.

- Jesus agonized in prayer over dying for our sins.

- The disciples slept.

- Jesus committed himself to do his Father's will, no matter what the cost.

What does this incident teach you about prayer and God's will?

- Prayer can be a struggle with God, yet it can also help us accept God's will.

- Sometimes prayer is difficult, and we don't always get exactly what we want.

- God wants us to pray, even if only to pour out our hearts to him.

6 The betrayal and arrest of Jesus

How was Jesus arrested? (Matthew 26:47-56)

Judas came, singled out Jesus, and the soldiers seized him. Jesus did not allow Peter to use force to stop the arrest.

What does it mean to betray or desert Jesus?

- To give up your beliefs

- To fail to take a stand for him when opposed

- To say no to God's will

7 Jesus' trial before Caiaphas

What is noteworthy about Jesus' trial before the high priest? (Matthew 26:57-68)

- Jesus' silence—he did not defend himself.

- Jesus spoke only after the high priest demanded that he say whether he was the Son of God.

- The trial was rigged—the outcome was determined ahead of time.

Note: Jesus quoted from Daniel 7:13, claiming the title, "Son of Man." This was a name for the Messiah. By both agreeing with the "charge" and quoting this passage, Jesus' claims were unmistakable.

When is it better to say nothing than to defend yourself?

Encourage your group to explore various settings: home, church, work, and the world.

Note: Jesus had nothing to prove—he had already demonstrated his identity to everyone with his deeds and teachings. So he entrusted himself to God.

8   Peter's denial

What human tendencies do you see in Peter's denial of Christ? (Matthew 26:69-75)

- He followed Christ when it was popular.

- He succumbed to fear when pressed to identify with Christ.

- He failed to do what he promised to do.

- He let someone else intimidate him.

How do believers today deny Christ, whether they realize it or not?

When we are embarrassed or ashamed to let others know we are followers of Jesus.

In summary, what have you learned about Jesus' commitment to the Father's will?

Invite everyone to answer. Here are some possibilities:

- He was totally committed to his Father's will, even to the point of death.

- He sought (and gained) strength through prayer.

- He did not desert his friends, even though they deserted him.

- He trusted God in his suffering.

What have you learned about your own commitment to God's will?

Some possibilities:

- Following God's will has costs.

- I need to pray in times of need.

- I am prone to sinning even though I know Christ is in me.

- Even the strongest person can become weak and frightened.

Following Jesus means his prayer
becomes our own: "Your will be done."

YOUR WALK WITH GOD

Bible

Read Matthew 27 three times, noting observations and applications.

Prayer

Day One: Adoration—Read Isaiah 53, then write a prayer of adoration, worshipping God for the gift of his Son.

Day Two: Confession—Take a look back over the last month of your life. List the sins you remember being guilty of committing. List the acts of obedience you have been guilty of *not* doing. Confess these to God.

Day Three: Thanksgiving—Go over your list of confessions and write "Paid in full" next to every sin. Thank God for forgiving each and every sin and for accepting you through his grace.

Scripture Memory

Going a little farther, he fell with his face to the ground and prayed, "My Father, if it is possible, may this cup be taken from me. Yet not as I will, but as you will." Matthew 26:39

The theme of the next study is the crucifixion and death of Jesus. To prepare for the study, complete the assignment found in the On Your Own section.

PRAYER

Close the meeting with prayer.

Note: You will need to complete the following assignment before you come to the next meeting.

It is the first century A.D. You are a reporter for the *Jerusalem Gazette*. You have been assigned by your editor to go out and get the real story on Jesus. You are to list accurately all the details found in Matthew 27. But because you readers want more than the facts, you have to explain to them the significance of the facts you uncover. In other words, they want to know, "Why is this important?"

Take a piece of paper and divide it into two columns (shown below). List the facts on the left and your thoughts, insights, and applications on the right. Try to come up with at least four key facts and observations from Matthew 27.

Facts of the Story   **Insights and Applications**

The Crucifixion

10

OVERVIEW

The purpose of this study is to help group members grasp the magnitude of Christ's sacrifice for them.

Outside of Christ's resurrection, the Crucifixion was one of the most significant events in all of history. Believers who are familiar with the details of the story may miss appreciating its importance. Allow the account of Jesus' trial and crucifixion to impact you as you prepare for the study so you can carry that renewed perspective into the meeting.

PRAYER

Open the meeting with prayer. Invite God to move powerfully among you as you meditate on this most significant event.

REVIEW

Bible

Save the discussion of Matthew 27 for the lesson.

Prayer

Adoration: Have several people read the prayers they wrote in response to Isaiah 53.

Confession: Have each person share one or two requests concerning his or her spiritual life.

Thanksgiving: Ask the group, **What impact did it have on you to thank God for forgiving you of sin?**

Scripture Memory

Have everyone recite Matthew 26:39.

PURPOSE

Christ's death is one of the most important topics you can study as a Christian. More than just a painful death, the Crucifixion was Christ's act of paying for *your sins*. He was mocked, humiliated, and rejected in paying for *your* guilt. It is easy to think of Christ's death only as an event that happened in the past. But if it weren't for Christ's death, your life today would not be what it is.

As you read the story of Christ's death, imagine the scenes in your mind—see the soldiers' dirty faces, hear their sarcastic taunts, feel the marketplace heat, imagine the thorns digging into Jesus' head, and so on. Try to imagine what it must have been like for Jesus to go through the suffering he faced. Put yourself right next to it all.

In this study, you will learn about the price Jesus paid—the suffering and humiliation he endured for your benefit.

Reporting the Facts

Turn to your assignment from the previous study. As a reporter, what two facts and observations from the account in Matthew 27 were most striking to you?

Begin by having the group members identify a detail or fact and follow that with any insights and applications that flow from the information. Encourage each person to contribute at least one fact and application. It should be obvious that every fact and observation cannot be emphasized in one study time. By way of preparation, you need to ask yourself, "What events do I need to highlight for my group members? What will give them the best handles on the significance of the chapter of Scripture? What applications do they need stressed in their lives?" Draw out those key points and touch only lightly on the others.

We provide below a list of the key facts of the story as a reference. Observations are in italics.

The religious leaders plan to kill Jesus (v. 1). *It is hard to imagine the religious leaders in a community getting together to arrange a murder!*

Jesus delivered to Pilate (v. 2). *The leaders wanted another authority to put Jesus to death legally since they weren't allowed to execute a criminal without approval from Roman officials.*

Judas returns the money and hangs himself (vv. 3-5). *Judas's plans failed or he had some regret about what he had done. Note: While Judas acknowledged his sin, he failed to repent of it.*

Money used buy the potter's field (vv. 6-7). *Even though the chief priests wouldn't allow the tainted money in the temple, they refused to acknowledge their own sinful behavior in God's dwelling. Another prophecy has been fulfilled in these verses.*

Jesus stands before Pilate (vv. 11-14). *Committed to God's will, Jesus has resigned himself to their abuse. Also observe their hatred of Christ—people can (and do) hate him.*

Pilate's wife's dream (v. 19). *God will use a variety of means to show sinful people their errors.*

Choice of Barabbas (vv. 20-21). *Their envy of Jesus was so great that they wanted to free a murderer to ensure that Jesus would be executed.*

Call for Jesus' crucifixion (vv. 22-23). *The crowd doesn't have a reason for wanting Jesus' death—their hate is demonic. Also Pilate knows Jesus is innocent. This pagan had more insight into Christ than the "religious" people.*

Pilate washes his hands (v. 24). *Though recognizing the injustice, Pilate steps back and allows the mob to prevail.*

Jesus mocked by the soldiers (vv. 27-31). *What utter humiliation! Our experiences of being mocked or teased seem minor when compared to this incident.*

The crucifixion (vv. 35-50). *Jesus suffers greatly in his final hours and is abused by those around him. It seems too that creation has responded to Jesus' agony (v. 45).*

Temple curtain torn (v. 51). *The temple veil, which separated God from mankind in the Holy of Holies, is torn from top to bottom. No human being could have torn the curtain in that manner, making it clear that Christ, through his death, had brought about our access to God.*

Holy people raised in their tombs (vv. 52-53). *Jesus' death brings life!*

Centurion acknowledges Jesus as the Son of God (v. 54). *Once again, a pagan understands better than all of Israel what is happening here.*

Pharisees and chief priests try to "keep a good man down" (vv. 62-64). *The Resurrection was known before the fact even to Jesus' enemies.*

Guards set, tomb sealed (vv. 65-66). *This action ruled out the possibility that the disciples would steal Jesus' corpse and then claim that he had been resurrected.*

Jesus' Public Humiliation

What do you remember as one of your most painful experiences of rejection?

Have each person describe his or her feelings. Examples might include being teased in grade school, being cut from a team, failing a class, or being scorned by a parent.

What are some of the specific sufferings that Jesus endured at his public trial? (Matthew 27:11-26)

- He was accused of blasphemy by the religious leaders.

- The crowd asked for a criminal (Barabbas) to be released instead of Jesus.

- The crowd called for Jesus' execution.

- He was flogged—a particularly cruel punishment of being beaten severely with a whip. Many times it resulted in the death of the victim.

How did the soldiers cause Jesus to suffer? (Matthew 27:27-31)

- Stripped him.
- Put a scarlet robe on him.
- Put a crown of thorns on his head.
- Gave him a reed "scepter."
- Knelt down in mock adulation.
- Spat on him.
- Beat his head.
- Took off his robe.

What emotions do these scenes evoke in you?

Invite group members to answer. If appropriate, ask for more definition.

Jesus' Suffering on the Cross

What sufferings did Jesus endure on the cross? (Matthew 27:35-50)

- He was treated with contempt by the soldiers who divided his garments.
- He was mocked by passers-by.
- The sign above him made fun of his claims to be the king of the Jews.
- He was crucified—a form of execution reserved for criminals.
- He was crucified alongside criminals.
- None of his disciples defended him.
- He was nailed to the cross and stabbed in the side.
- The Father placed the world's sins on him and forsook him.

Note: While it is not necessarily obvious from the Gospel accounts, Jesus' chief suffering on the cross was not physical, but spiritual. As the perfect, sinless Son of God, he (1) took on the sins of the whole world, and (2) experienced separation from the Father. None of us will ever fully know what that kind of suffering meant, but it was real and it was costly.

What emotions does this scene evoke in you?

Invite everyone to respond.

What was most significant to you about Jesus' death on the cross?

This was where Jesus actually paid the price for our sin. He experienced separation from God—for the first time in eternity—while on the cross, and there he gave up his life.

Jesus' Death and Burial

What events happened right after the Crucifixion? (Matthew 27:51-66)

- Some dead people came to life (27:52-53).

- Centurion acknowledged Jesus as the Son of God as women looked on (27:54-56).

- Joseph asked for the body of Jesus (27:57-58).

- Joseph prepared Jesus for burial and laid him in his tomb (27:59-60).

- Pharisees and chief priests arranged for sealing of the tomb (27:62-64).

- Guards set, and tomb sealed (27:65-66).

If time permits, ask how each person feels about what has just been discussed. What are their gut reactions to how Jesus suffered? What will they remember when they wake up the next morning?

BOTTOM LINE

Following Christ means valuing the Crucifixion as God's greatest demonstration of his love for you.

YOUR WALK WITH GOD

Bible

Read Matthew 28 three times.

Prayer

Day One: Adoration—Write a prayer in answer to the question, "What if Jesus had not been raised from the dead?" For example: "Father, if Jesus had not been raised from the dead, I _____ and you _____." Or: "Lord, I worship you for the resurrection of Jesus, because otherwise _____."

Day Two: Confession—In what specific ways do you demonstrate a lack of faith—perhaps a worry that you need to entrust to God? Confess this and pray that God will increase your faith.

Day Three: Supplication—Pray by name for three unsaved friends.

Scripture Memory

But God demonstrates his own love for us in this: While we were still sinners, Christ died for us. Romans 5:8

Our next study will focus on the Resurrection. Why is this event central to Christianity? How do our Easter celebrations highlight or miss this important event?

PRAYER

Close the meeting with prayer.

ON YOUR OWN

Read and study the account of the resurrection of Jesus in each of the Gospels:

Matthew 28:1-15

Mark 16:1-14

Luke 24:1-49

John 20:1-31

What facts appear in all four Gospel accounts?

What facts appear in at least two of the Gospel accounts? (List which Gospels contain each fact.)

What facts appear in only one Gospel account?

11

The Resurrection

The purpose of this study is to help group members understand the importance of Jesus' resurrection.

In this study, avoid trying to prove the facts of the Resurrection unless your group members have specific questions. If they do, you'll find some extra information under the heading "On Your Own" at the end of the study. Otherwise, focus discussion on why the Resurrection is important to their faith.

PRAYER

Open the meeting with prayer.

REVIEW

Bible

Invite group members to share observations and applications from Matthew 28.

Prayer

Adoration: Have each group member read his or her prayer of adoration.

Confession: Ask the group, **What is one worry that you have turned over to God?**

Supplication: Find out if any group members were not able to identify three non-Christian friends; take this time to help identify them.

Scripture Memory

Have everyone recite Romans 5:8.

PURPOSE

In our secular culture, Easter lives in the shadows of other holidays. Compared to Christmas, for example, Easter hardly makes an appearance. In most churches this is not the case, but for the vast majority of modern men and women, Easter comes and goes without much fanfare.

Yet Christ's resurrection is a pivotal event. It is absolutely central to the Christian faith. You could not be a Christian without it being true. Our salvation stands or falls with the resurrection of Jesus. Without the Resurrection, Christianity is just one more religion. The Resurrection declares that faith in Christ is a personal encounter with the living God, not just a philosophy, a set of morals, or the teachings of a spiritual leader. The Resurrection declares the deity of Jesus Christ, God among us, all-powerful and triumphant over sin. It tells us that God came, took away our sins, and invited us to receive forgiveness.

In this study, we will focus our attention on what makes the Resurrection so significant.

STUDY

The Resurrection is recorded in all four Gospels: Matthew 28:1-15; Mark 16:1-14; Luke 24:1-49; John 20:1-31. Turn to the assignment you prepared for this study to answer the questions below.

Jesus Rose from the Dead

What facts appear in all four Gospel accounts?

- The Resurrection took place on the first day of the week (fulfilling Jesus' prophecy that he would rise on the third day by Jewish reckoning of time).

- Mary Magdalene was among the first to arrive at the tomb.

- Jesus was not in the tomb.

- The stone had been moved.

- An angel was present at Mary's arrival.

- The disciples were skeptical about the Resurrection at first.

- Once Jesus appeared to the Eleven, they believed.

What do we gain from having four different accounts of this event?

Each brings a different perspective and emphasizes different facts, like four different reporters covering the same event. They tell the story . . .

- from four different perspectives.

- at four different times.

- for four different reasons.

- to four different audiences.

For example, Matthew, who wrote to the Jews, noted the religious leaders bribing the guards. He included what helped him drive home the point about the corrupted nature of the religious establishment. John, on the other hand, who had a sensitive temperament, noted the disciples' reactions more often than the other Gospel writers. Each writer selected the details that helped make his particular emphasis.

The Significance of the Resurrection

What makes the Resurrection significant to our faith? (1 Corinthians 15:12-19)

If the Resurrection did not happen, several conclusions follow:

- Our preaching is in vain (15:14).

- We are liars for claiming that God raises people from the dead (15:15).

- We're still in our sins, unredeemed, guilty before God, and deserving of condemnation (15:17).

- Dead believers are dead forever, never to be alive again (15:18).

- Every Christian should be pitied as a fool for throwing away his or her life on something that isn't real (15:19).

Note: If you have time, you can also note other key ideas mentioned later in 1 Corinthians:

- The Resurrection undid what Adam's sin did (15:22).

- The Resurrection can inspire us to endure trying circumstances (15:31-32).

- The fact of the Resurrection leaves us with the promise of perfect bodies in heaven (15:42-44).

- The Resurrection can inspire us to be steadfast and diligent in God's work (15:58).

What implications does Christ's resurrection have for our understanding about life after death? (1 Corinthians 15:29-32, 35-54)

All Christians will be raised from the dead—that is, their physical bodies will be changed into permanent spiritual ones—just as Christ was raised.

Note: The Greeks already had a concept of spiritual afterlife; what was foolishness to them was the Hebrew concept of dead bodies somehow being rebuilt from their decayed state into functioning people again. The first body's relationship to the second body is like the relationship of a seed to the final plant (1 Corinthians 15:37)—the second comes from the first, but they're as different as a stalk is from the original grain of wheat. Genetically, the seed and the plant are identical; but their appearance and function are different.

How does the Resurrection give us hope?

- It gives us hope for the future.

- It gives us hope for those who die in Christ.

- It gives us a reason to tell others about Christ.

- We know we will live forever.

- We know we will be rewarded for serving Christ.

How does Christ's death on the cross and his resurrection especially touch you?

Probe for their reasons if appropriate.

Following Jesus means recognizing the meaning
and hope his resurrection has for us.

Bible

Read Acts 1 three times.

Prayer

Day One: Adoration—From your memory of all you've learned in *"Follow Me!"* make a list of all that the praiseworthy deeds Jesus did as a man on earth. Praise him for his deeds.

Day Two: Confession—Ask God to bring to mind sins of which you have not been aware, and confess these to him.

Day Three: Supplication—Continue to pray for your three unsaved friends.

Scripture Memory

Therefore, my dear brothers, stand firm. Let nothing move you. Always give yourselves fully to the work of the Lord, because you know that your labor in the Lord is not in vain. 1 Corinthians 15:58

In the next study we will take a closer look at Jesus' final words to his followers—the Great Commission. What do you think Jesus wanted to impress upon his disciples at that point?

Close the meeting with prayer.

Reading the different accounts of the Resurrection may raise questions about why the Gospels differ in the various details of the story. For example, you may wonder:

Was there one angel or two?

How many women went to the tomb?

Were the angels outside or inside the tomb?

Who actually went into the tomb?

Did Peter go *into* the tomb, or just look in?

Those kinds of questions may lead to deeper ones:

Why didn't God cause the writers to report the details exactly alike?

Isn't the Bible infallible and inerrant?

How can we explain the apparent contradictions between the Gospels?

The following three principles may help you as you ponder such questions.

1 Differences from one narrative to another arise because each writer left out some details.

A true contradiction between the Gospel accounts is actually harder to find than you might think. For example, does John's comment in John 20:1 that Mary Magdalene went to the tomb, with no mention of any other women going with her, rule out the possibility that other women were with her but just not mentioned? Not at all. His story doesn't really contradict the others—it just doesn't say everything. We have a hint of this in John 20:2, where Mary says "we"; even in John there's a hint that she was not alone.

In other words, facts left out of one account but not another do not necessarily indicate a contradiction between the two. A true contradiction would be a statement such as, "And Mary Magdalene came early to the tomb alone—no one was with her." No such contradictory statements exist in the Gospels.

Consider the following story. A woman was waiting for a bus with a friend. As the bus approached, the crowd pressed forward and she was pushed in the path of the bus. The bus struck her and an ambulance was called. Meanwhile, the friend called the woman's husband and told him, "Your wife has been hit by a bus. I'll call you when we find out what hospital she's been taken to." About an hour later, the husband received another call. This time it was a police officer. "I'm sorry to inform you Sir, but your wife has just been killed in a car accident." When the man expressed his shock that he had heard her injuries from being hit by the bus were not that severe, the officer replied that there was no bus involved and that she had been killed while a passenger in an automobile.

From the looks of the above story, the police officer and the friend are contradicting each other. Somebody is mistaken on what vehicles were involved and the nature of the woman's injuries (or else one or both of those people called the wrong husband!). In any event, if we were reading this account in two different newspapers (one story from the officer and one story from the friend) it is hard not to assume the accounts are mixed up. If you read those stories, you'd want to ask some more questions to find out what really went on.

As it turns out both the friend and the police officer were one hundred percent correct in every detail. The woman had been hit by a bus. Before the ambulance arrived, a passerby offered to take her to the hospital. While en route in that car, the woman was involved in the fatal auto accident. The two stories can be completely harmonized omitting nothing. Had someone tampered with either story to erase the contradiction, the final story would not have been true to the actual events. So leaving the stories as they are, even with apparent contradictions, is a more honest and credible option. That is how the Gospels come to us. In many cases they can be made to complement each other without negating each other.

2 Differences often authenticate a story because they prove there has been no attempt to change the details in order to harmonize the accounts.

When faced with a possible contradiction, even generally honest people may fudge some of the details to make stories fit. This is especially true of dishonest people. But in the New Testament we don't see this adjusting going on—the writers told their stories as they saw them (or heard them).

And as we said above, the contradictions may not turn out to be real contradictions after all.

3 Scripture is God-breathed, and God is incapable of falsehood.

We say the Bible is without error because any book from God (as fulfilled prophecy and its incredible trustworthiness show that it is) would have to be utterly and completely truthful. God cannot lie, nor can he mix truth with error. And if God says something through a prophet, it will always and in every case be true because God is speaking and he cannot speak falsely.

No prophet speaking by God's Spirit ever uttered a falsehood. "No prophecy of Scripture came about by the prophet's own interpretation. For prophecy never had its origin in the will of man, but men spoke from God as they were carried along by the Holy Spirit" (2 Peter 1:20-21). If the Scriptures are God's Word, they contain no errors.

What then should we do when we come upon an apparent contradiction or mistake? We recognize them as such and try to solve them. Harmonize the accounts or admit we don't know. But one option we don't have is to impute error to God. Once we say that God inspired error, we open the door to anything in the Bible being a possible mistake. If God ever told one lie, he could have told a thousand. But our God never has, and never will, tell us something that isn't true. That is why difficulties in Scripture don't change its inerrancy, because we anchor our hope of pure truth in his nature and recognize that such problems will ultimately have a solution.

Jesus had this view of Scripture. A quick survey of the Gospels will reveal his tremendous respect for its truth. Statements such as, "The Scripture cannot be broken" (John 10:35), and, "Since you do not believe what [Moses] wrote, how are you going to believe what I say?" (John 5:47) show his trust in and high view of the operation of God's Spirit in the Bible.

If Jesus is Lord of our lives, he is Lord of our beliefs. And he believed in the invulnerability and utter truthfulness of Scripture; to call him Lord then is to agree with him about the nature of the Bible.

The accounts of Jesus' resurrection do differ. But their apparent contradictions are really just that—apparent. Our finite minds will have to wait for a full disclosure of details that will resolve all our questions. But based on who God is and in submission to the authority of Christ, we do not impute error to God, and we fully anticipate the answer to our every question that will show God's complete and eternal truthfulness.

The Call
(Great Commission)

OVERVIEW

The purpose of this study is to challenge group members to follow Jesus by making disciples.

Jesus calls us all to continue his mission of making disciples, but that doesn't imply that we are to make clones. We are to reach out and influence people to become "learners" and followers of Jesus, at the level we can and according to our varied abilities to do so. This study is an opportunity to challenge each of your group members to say, "Yes, Lord, I will follow you by helping others grow toward maturity."

PRAYER

Open the meeting with prayer.

REVIEW

Bible

Have group members share observations and applications from Acts 1.

Prayer

Adoration: Ask group members what praiseworthy deeds of Jesus' they listed.

Confession: Ask volunteers what new area of weakness God has revealed to them.

Supplication: Pray together for the unsaved friends that everyone has been praying for.

Scripture Memory

Have group members recite 1 Corinthians 15:58.

PURPOSE

Remember when people used to ask you, "What do you want to be when you grow up?" Whatever your answer to that question when you were younger, you probably had *some* reply. Even if you didn't have specific plans for the future, you knew that eventually you would become an adult. One day you would grow up.

To grow up is a mixed blessing. Adulthood brings new responsibilities as well as new opportunities. Not only can you do more, you're *expected* to do more. And like all change, adulthood brings you to more uncharted territory, making you unsure exactly what lies ahead. It's the same with being a Christian.

From among his many followers, Jesus chose twelve men to be with him all the time. It's true that he did this so they could learn for themselves, but there was also another reason: so they could learn how to teach others. Jesus wanted his disciples not only to become godly men, but also to become teachers of others. That meant, eventually, becoming disciple-makers themselves.

Jesus wants every Christian to mature to the point of making disciples. That means growing from a place of mere belief to that of persuading others to believe; helping new believers understand their faith; and encouraging other believers to follow him. In other words, following Jesus means passing on the faith to others—what is often called fulfilling the Great Commission.

In this study, we will explore what it means to fulfill the Great Commission.

The Call

Begin the study by telling the group that they are going to do something different this week. Select two people to read the following skit aloud while everyone else follows along. Tell the group to use their imaginations to place themselves in the role described.

Two important conditions should be announced before they begin reading:

1. No matter what their actual situation is now, they must try very hard to relate to the situation as described in the assignment. It may not fit their circumstances at all, so urge them to "pretend big" if they have to.

2. No matter how difficult it would be them to accept the assignment if it were a real one, they must do so for the sake of the exercise. They can't decline this offer!

The Scene: Imagine that you are the owner and president of a dynamic, medium-size company with about 50 employees. It's Tuesday night, about 8:30 P.M. You're sitting in your favorite living room chair. It's your first real moment today to rest and relax with your spouse. The work day is behind you and the kids are in bed. The phone rings and you reach to get it . . .

You: Hello?

Caller: Hello, is _____ there?

You: Yes, this is _____.

Caller: Are you sitting down?

You: Well, as a matter of fact I am.

Caller: That's good, because what I have to tell you may surprise you. This is the president of the United States calling.

You: Oh, sure it is . . . and I'm the Queen of England! Come on, who is this really?

Caller: This is no prank call. This is your president, and I am very serious about this. If you don't believe me, just look out your front door. You will find two men standing there in dark suits. They are Secret Service agents, and they will show you IDs if necessary.

You: OK, I'll check—and let me add, they had better be there.

(You go to the front door. Sure enough, two men in dark suits are standing there, just as he said. You ask for their IDs, and they show them. Suddenly you realize you have been rude to the president of the United States and have left him on hold! You rush back and pick up the receiver.)

You: Mr. President, I'm sorry, really . . . I just never expected in a million years to hear from you!

President: I understand.

You: What can I do for you, Sir?

President: Please listen. I have a matter of grave importance to communicate to you.

You: I'm all ears, Mr. President. Go ahead.

President: There is an issue of national security and world peace at stake and, though you may find this hard to believe, you are the only one—let me repeat that, the only one—who can help. The future of our country and the world is hanging in the balance. I need you. We need you. The world needs you. Do you want me to continue.

You: Oh yes, Mr. President, anything I can do for my country.

President: I am glad you are willing. I cannot stress enough that you are the only one we can count on.

You: I understand, Mr. President. What can I do?

President: We need you to go on a mission, a top secret mission. You will not know where you are going until you are at the Air Force base awaiting takeoff.

You: It sounds very exciting, sir. Tell me more.

President: Well, there is one major catch, and as we see it, no way around it.

You: What's that, Sir?

President: The mission will take ten years, during which you will be completely unable to contact any friends or loved ones.

You: Wow! That is a catch!

President: We will give you one year to prepare yourself, your family, and your business for your absence. Your departure date is set for one year from today. I will have my people get in touch with you to help you in any way possible. Please plan carefully and thoughtfully, as you will have no contact with the life you now have for ten years. You will receive a packet of information shortly with all the necessary details. I will also call back to see how preparations are going. Until then, thank you. The world will perhaps never know just how significant a role you played in its destiny.

If you were this business owner, what would you do to ensure that the corporation maintains the same superior performance in your absence?

Give the group a few moments to collect their thoughts, and then allow as many people as time allows to suggest answers. When they are finished, emphasize these three points. *First, as owner, you should find someone to carry on your business.* You want others to be able to step into your shoes so that the business runs as though you were there. *Second, the individuals you train must be selected carefully.* You should spend considerable thought and prayer in choosing someone. You might even create a detailed list that spells out the qualities and skills you would want to see in the people who are assuming your job. *Finally, you must see to it that those carefully selected people are carefully trained.* If they are going to duplicate your leadership, then they will have to know you well and observe what it is that makes you unique.

Then point out that Jesus essentially followed these three steps when he prepared the disciples for their important lifelong mission. The remainder of the study will show your group that Jesus' careful training of the Twelve was essential to their successful evangelism later.

How Jesus Made Disciples

1   Focused on a Few

How many disciples did Jesus train closely? (Mark 3:14-19)

Twelve.

Many more than these twelve men followed Jesus. The women who supported him, the seventy-two whom he sent out two by two, and whole crowds of admirers were all true disciples of Jesus. But Jesus focused his efforts on these twelve. And he deliberately chose them for that purpose.

2   Selected Them Carefully

How did Jesus choose the twelve with whom he worked closely? (Luke 6:12-13)

Soon after Jesus began ministering, he prayed and choose them from among his many followers.

Note: Jesus prayed all night before selecting the Twelve.

3 Trained Them

Why did Jesus choose the Twelve? (Mark 3:13-14)

> So they could be with him and preach.

> Note: From among all Jesus' disciples, only these twelve traveled with him, literally following him everywhere he went. They were Jesus' inner circle and had access to him much more than the mass of casual followers. Jesus invested most of his time and energy in these twelve.

What purpose did Jesus have in sending his disciples out to preach? (Mark 3:13-14)

> He was training them to take over his ministry.

> Note: Jesus' message was eventually going to be entrusted entirely to the care of his twelve disciples, who would in turn do the same with the new believers that came after them.

What final mission did Jesus give his twelve disciples? (Matthew 28:18-20)

> He entrusted them with making new disciples.

What tasks does this "Great Commission" require of all Christians living today? (Matthew 28:18-20)

> - To tell unbelievers about Christ
> - To help new believers grow
> - To encourage other Christians to obey God

How can your unique gifts and abilities be used in making disciples for Christ?

> Invite each person to answer.

Life Dedicated to the Great Commission

1 Home

In what ways can you disciple your family?

> - Set a good example.
> - Talk about current events and what the Bible says to them.
> - Hold family devotions.
> - Serve by doing chores and other dirty work.

2 Church

In what way can you be a disciple-maker in your local church?

> Lead a small group, encourage other leaders, support the staff who oversee small groups, and so on.

3 Friends

What coworkers, neighbors, or friends can you serve as Christ's messenger?

> Ask group members how they might be able to reach these people.

4 World

In what ways can do you think discipling others will eventually impact the world?

> As ripples spread out in a pond, the people we disciple will disciple others, and if that continues, the whole world will eventually be reached.

What is one change you could make in your life to better fulfill Jesus' call to make disciples?

> Invite volunteers to respond.

BOTTOM LINE

Following Jesus means helping fulfill the Great Commission.

YOUR WALK WITH GOD

Bible

Read Acts 2 three times, noting observations and applications.

Prayer

Day One: Adoration—Make a list of the truths about Jesus that have changed your life in some way.

Day Two: Confession—Ask God to forgive any hardness or insensitivity you may have had toward Christ.

Day Three: Supplication—Write out a prayer of devotion to Jesus, asking God to make you a better follower each day.

Scripture Memory

Review the following verses: Matthew 26:39; Romans 5:8; 1 Corinthians 15:58.

The next study will be a review of the book. Take a look back through the pages of this study guide and think about the most important insights you have gained, and how these truths have impacted your life.

PRAYER

Close the meeting with prayer.

Reviewing "Follow Me!"

OVERVIEW

The purpose of this study is to help your group members assess what they've learned about following Jesus.

The final study of *"Follow Me!"* will give your group members an opportunity to review the insights they've gained about following Christ.

REVIEW

Bible

Have the group share observations and applications from Acts 2.

Prayer

Adoration—Ask what truths about Jesus have changed your group members the most.

Confession—Ask how group members have been made more sensitive to Christ over the last twelve weeks.

Supplication—Have everyone share the requests they made of God. Pray for each other using these requests.

Scripture Memory

Have various group members recite Matthew 26:39; Romans 5:8; 1 Corinthians 15:58.

This review culminates your study of *"Follow Me!"* the third book in the *Walking With God Series*. Use this time to reflect on your experience and to summarize what you've learned about following Jesus.

As you know by now, following Christ is more than just a matter of believing in Jesus. It is a personal relationship with him, involving prayer, worship, and trust. This review invites you to look back on what you've learned over the last twelve weeks and apply it to that ongoing relationship.

STUDY

Discoveries about Following Jesus

During the past twelve weeks, what has been your most meaningful insight about following Christ?

Invite everyone to share.

What does it mean to do everything to the glory of God?

It means to try to honor God in everything you do.

What is one area of your life that you have submitted to the lordship of Christ as a result of this study?

Areas of life could include money, friendships, dating, popularity, work habits, family life, plans for the future, and so on.

What are some ways a Christian should serve Christ with money and possessions?

Giving to the poor, tithing, letting others borrow from you, and so on.

What are some benefits you receive as a result of following Jesus?

> Increased faith, hope for the future, changed character, and so on.

How have you had to adjust your expectations of God?

> For example, he will not necessarily give us an easy life.

In what way does opposition to your faith challenge you?

> It strengthens us and helps us depend on Jesus more completely.

What do you need to do to ready yourself for Jesus' return?

> Simplify my life here and now so I can concentrate on that which lasts forever.

What about doing God's will do you find most difficult?

> Answers could include putting our own desires aside, obeying certain commands, avoiding certain sins, or accepting certain people.

What is most meaningful to you about Christ's death?

> His love for us, his sacrifice of atonement, and so on.

Why is it significant that Jesus rose from the dead?

> This makes our salvation real and gives us certainty of eternal life.

What can you do at this time in your life to help fulfill the Great Commission?

> Begin to identify two or three people to whom you can invest yourself.

BOTTOM LINE

Following Jesus is what the Christian life is all about.

YOUR WALK WITH GOD

Bible

Read the book of Mark through in order to capture a sense of Jesus' life and its life-changing, world-changing, history-changing, and eternity-changing impact.

Prayer

Day One: Adoration—Weather permitting, go for a walk or bike ride and pray out loud. If the weather isn't cooperative, find a place of solitude indoors where you can pray out loud, praising Jesus for who he is—our Lord and Savior.

Day Two: Thanksgiving—What ministries or people have contributed to your spiritual growth? Thank God for them each by name.

Day Three: Supplication—Pray for at least one specific area of ministry in the church—what are their needs? How can those ministries do better? What do the leaders need? How might Satan be trying to destroy what God is doing there?

Scripture Memory

Review all of the verses you've memorized in *"Follow Me!"*: Luke 6:46; 1 Corinthians 10:31; Matthew 16:24; 1 Corinthians 9:25; Matthew 16:25; Luke 6:22; Matthew 26:39; Romans 5:8; 1 Corinthians 15:58.

PRAYER

You or any member of the group should close in prayer.

ON YOUR OWN

Arrange a time to sit down with each group member individually over the next few weeks. (If your group is a couples group, have men meet with men, women with women, or couples with couples.) Have them discuss their perspectives on their spiritual growth as measured by the four categories listed below.

Self-Evaluation

Your group leader will be meeting with you to discuss your current spiritual condition and your hopes for growing in your faith. Please take some time to reflect honestly on where you stand right now within these four basic categories of Christian growth. Rate yourself in each category.

+   Doing well. I'm pleased with my progress so far.

✓   On the right track, but I see definite areas for improvement.

—   This is a struggle. I need some help.

A Disciple Is One Who . . .

Walks with God

To what extent is my Bible study and prayer time adequate for helping me walk with God?

Rating:

Comments:

Lives the Word

To what extent is my mind filled with scriptural truths so that my actions and reactions show I am being transformed?

Rating:

Comments:

Contributes to the work

To what extent am I actively participating in the church with my time, talents, and treasures.

Rating:

Comments:

Impacts the world

To what extent am I impacting my world with a Christian witness and influence?

Rating:

Comments:

Other issues I would like to discuss with my small group leader:

The *Walking With God Journal* is the perfect companion to the *Walking With God Series*. Use it to keep your notes during Bible study, record your prayers, or simply jot down your thoughts and insights. (0-310-91642-9)

NOTES